Jil from
Karen

MARION CONLIN'S COOKING SCHOOL

MARION CONLIN'S COOKING SCHOOL

By Marion Conlin

Illustrated by Henning Jensen

DILLON PRESS, INC., MINNEAPOLIS, MINNESOTA

©1972 by Dillon Press, Inc. All rights reserved

Dillon Press, Inc.
Minneapolis, Minnesota 55401

International Standard Book Number: 0-87518-047-7
Library of Congress Catalog Card Number: 74-187130

Printed in the United States of America

Except for brief sections quoted for review purposes, no part or parts of this book may be reproduced without written permission from the publisher.

TABLE OF CONTENTS

Introduction	vii
Eye-Openers for Morning People	1
Salad-Plus Menus	21
His and Her Special Menus	43
All Aboard: Passports, Please	63
Lotus Bowl Imports	87
Amigos de Mexico	111
Buon Gusto Italiano	131
Bistro Suppers by Candlelight	155
Dining Out at Home: Continental Style	179
Index	207

INTRODUCTION

Welcome to my Kitchen Cooking School! For many years, my classes have been filled with homemakers who are eager to improve their cooking skills and become more confident in the art of entertaining.

In an attempt to meet the needs of my enthusiastic students, I have organized actual cooking school lessons into a simplified textbook of practical menus. As you use the book, you will quickly see that each lesson is a total menu, guiding you step-by-step through cooking techniques. You won't have to brace yourself for a hard-to-follow lecture and then a trial period where ingredients are reduced to rubble and you are reduced to tears. Instead, success has been programmed into these recipes by students who have tested and retested them in my classes. Because of their experiences, you too can turn out a beautiful menu the very first time you try!

While cooking your way through each menu, you'll find that utensils and cooking methods have been geared to the American kitchen. Convenience foods are used to allow you an acceptable compromise between limited time and your wish to produce, with ease, the great classic dishes of the world. Most recipes have been divided into two major steps of preparation: *advance* and *final*. All recipes are sufficient for six to eight adults, unless otherwise indicated. Wine and beverage suggestions, as well as ideas for final presentation, accompany the menus.

Thus, in your own home you will be attending my Kitchen Cooking School. I suggest that on your own, or with a group of friends, you cook your way through the book. Use one menu at a time as a learning experience or as a menu for entertaining. Each contains recipes, techniques, and related information as it is presented in my kitchen classes. You need not be afraid of even those menus which sound the most complicated. Instead, you can be confident in the knowledge that all of the recipes have been prepared countless times in classes by persons with varying levels of cooking experience.

To maintain authenticity in the many foreign cuisines, you may find it helpful to do as my students and I do. We search out foreign grocery stores. I suggest you do the same. Check with local specialty restaurants as well. Their supplies come from somewhere, and you'll be surprised at what you can find at your own doorstep! Most store and restaurant owners are pleased to find someone interested in their native foods, and are more than cooperative in assisting you in your search for ingredients. When traveling, make it a habit to check the Yellow Pages for stores stocking hard-to-find items.

Within each chapter dealing with a specific cuisine, you are urged to mix-and-match recipes to create your own menu combinations. A word of caution: do not cross cultural boundaries in a single menu.

In planning for a party, consider creating an atmosphere that restates the cultural origin of the menu. Plan a table setting with a centerpiece of fresh fruit or vegetables, or even utensils from your kitchen which are appropriate to the cuisine. What a refreshing change from the typical starched white tablecloths and rigid floral arrangements! I also urge you to purchase an inexpensive set of white china. Such inexpensive white china has these advantages: it works well with vividly colored linen and a variety of accessories, it enhances the natural colors of the foods, and it can be warmed or chilled as necessary. Remember, warming and chilling dishes is the sign of a cook who cares.

Many men have now liberated themselves from the stereotyped male roles in cooking — salads, omelets, and charcoal broiled steaks. Instead, serious cooks, male or female, are now making soufflés and fine French stews. There is not a single recipe in this book that a gentleman gourmet wouldn't enjoy cooking.

Many gourmets who have developed a high regard for their palates now dispense with the cocktail hour altogether. Instead, they have found that a simple apértif before dinner, and a fine wine with dinner, provides unexpected sensory delights. When the cocktail hour is limited or dispensed with, children who are old enough to make valuable contributions and still too young for cocktails, may also be included on your guest list as they are in European homes.

My personal philosophy on pleasant dining and sharing warm convivial evenings with family or friends is based on including them "in" right from the beginning. It's a well-established tradition in our home that guests don aprons and ask what they can do. Together we chop, pound, filet, and sauté our way toward the final reward of sitting down and sharing a fine dining experience. I suggest you take the lead among your friends, or possibly a gourmet group, and do the same in your home. Using my book as a guide, let your guests, both men and women, join together for a happy and successful kitchen cooking school of your own.

I only wish every one of you could join my kitchen classes. A happy alternative can be yours by simply cooking your way through this book menu by menu. and sharing the experience with those you love!

Happy Cooking!

MARION CONLIN

MARION CONLIN'S COOKING SCHOOL

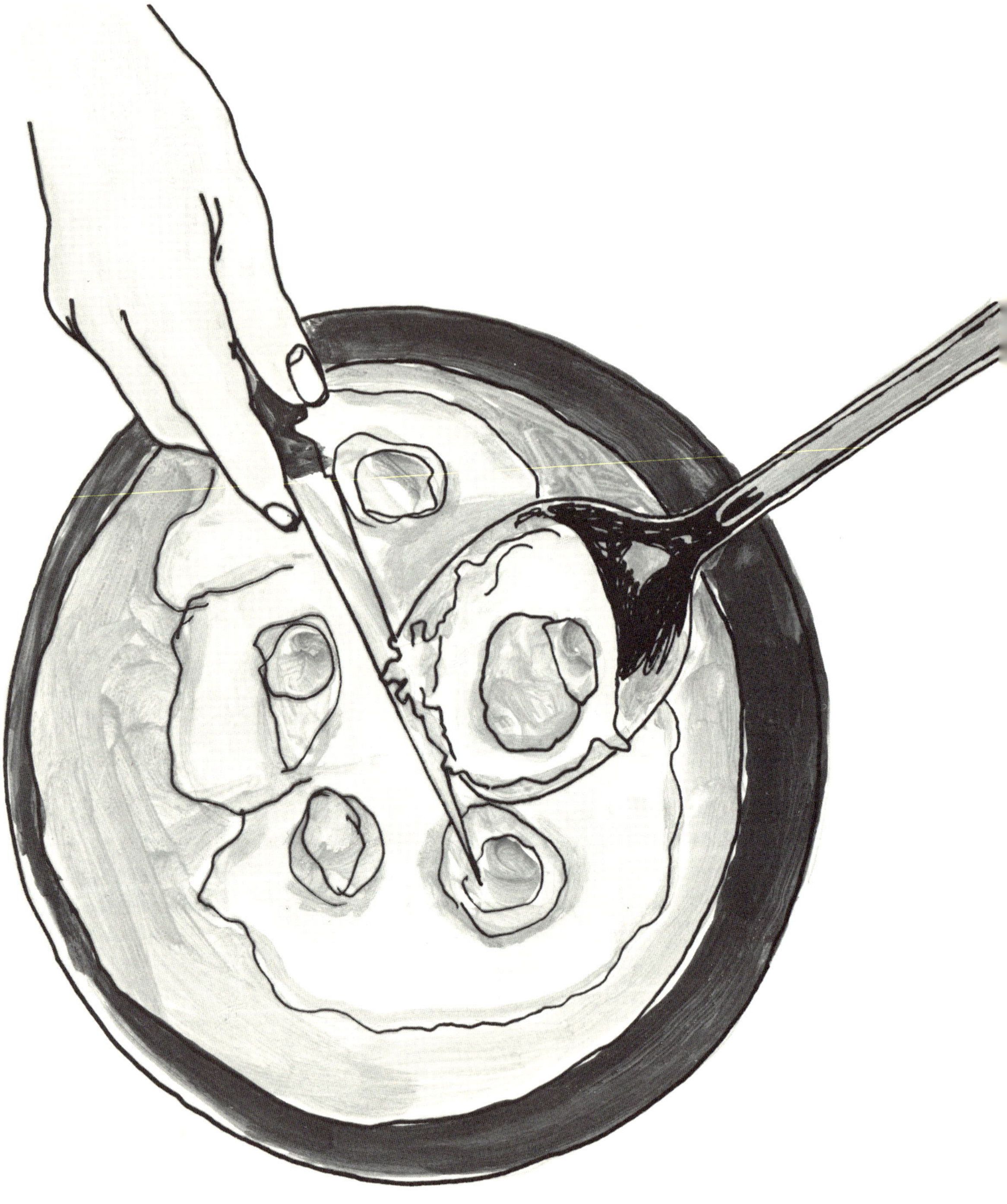

EYE-OPENERS FOR MORNING PEOPLE

What to cook when you've invited large numbers of people to breakfast, or when a family celebration is on the agenda before noon.

Grenadine Citrus Cup
Cottage Scrambled Eggs   Oven-Fried Farm Sausage
Brioche and Little Jars of Jam
Coffee

Most of us don't need any help when planning family breakfasts. As a matter of fact many of us feel that what we eat for breakfast is a personal matter. Rather like religion or our husband's income . . . it's not exactly hush-hush, but we don't enjoy being questioned about it.

But there are few of us who can escape without an occasional breakfast for guests. This is when we start thumbing through cookbooks and turning to our friends for advice. About the time we think we have come up with the world's most sophisticated menu, we might hear the man in our life say something like, "What's all the fuss about . . . we'll have scrambled eggs!" And as we sit there utterly undone, he adds, "with sausage, of course."

As the hostess at this sure-to-be-mundane affair, we then set out to give the menu a little jolt of creativity and some evidence of caring. The Grenadine citrus cup fills the creative requirement and pleases the busy hostess, as it can be fully prepared the night before. Brioche, that elegant breakfast bread invented by the French, gets across the message that you care. In this version, the dough is made ahead, shaped, and refrigerated over night. It only needs to be brushed with egg glaze and popped in the oven a few minutes before needed.

As simple as scrambling eggs might seem, it is not a procedure without pitfalls, particularly when working with large numbers of eggs. In cooking classes we have found a magic formula. It is simply beating cottage cheese into the eggs and cooking them in a non-stick skillet. Cottage cheese helps to keep the eggs fluffy and moist without "watering." The non-stick pan makes it possible to retrieve every speck of the finished product, cooked to perfection.

The components of this menu are rather "country" in feeling. To decorate your tables you might use calico tablecloths, lots of polished copper, and rustic field flowers. Antique baskets, jam jars, and crocks extend the country motif and turn this plain-Jane menu into a crowd-pleasing party breakfast.

This menu is planned for eight persons but it could easily be expanded to serve sixteen, or even twenty-four.

Grenadine Citrus Cup

Peel and section 3 Texas ruby-red grapefruit and 4 navel oranges. Place in container and add 2 cans frozen pineapple chunks. Add ¾ cup Grenadine. Cover and marinate overnight. In season, garnish with pomegranate seeds.

3 Texas ruby-red grapefruit
4 navel oranges
2 cans (13½-ounce) frozen pineapple chunks
¾ cup Grenadine
1 pomegranate, in season

Cottage Scrambled Eggs

(1) Beat together 12 eggs, 1 cup cream-style cottage cheese, 2 teaspoons salt, and ½ teaspoon black pepper.
(2) Heat 4 tablespoons butter in a non-stick electric frypan. When butter foams, add eggs and stir with rubber spatula from the bottom until eggs are set but remain slightly glossy.
(3) Transfer to chafing dish and sprinkle with finely minced parsley and chives.
(4) *Variation* For a change, stir ½ pound sliced sautéed mushrooms or a little minced fresh tarragon into Cottage Scrambled Eggs.

12 eggs
1 cup cream-style cottage cheese
2 teaspoons salt
½ teaspoon black pepper

4 tablespoons butter

2 tablespoons each minced parsley and chives

Oven-Fried Farm Sausage

Pre-heat oven to 375 degrees. Place 2 pounds link sausage in heavy iron skillet. Add ¼ cup sherry. Heat skillet on burner until sherry bubbles; then transfer to oven. Bake 30 minutes, turning after 15 minutes.

2 pounds link sausage
¼ cup sherry

Brioche (French Breakfast Rolls)

Advance Preparation (1) Measure 1 cup warm water into large mixer bowl. Dissolve 1 package active dry yeast in water. Add ¼ cup instant non-fat dry milk, ¼ cup sugar, ¼ cup softened butter, 2 eggs, 1 teaspoon salt and 1½ cups flour. Beat 3 minutes. Measure 2½ cups additional flour by spooning into cup and

1 cup warm water
1 package active dry yeast
¼ cup instant non-fat dry milk
¼ cup sugar
¼ cup butter, softened
2 eggs
1 teaspoon salt
4 cups all-purpose flour

3

leveling off. Continuing to beat, add as much of this flour as the mixer can comfortably handle. Add remaining flour and work into dough by hand, using a wooden spoon.

(2) Cover bowl and let stand 15 minutes. Remove to floured board and knead just briefly until dough is no longer sticky.

(3) Using three-fourths of the dough shape 12 small rounds which half fill each cup in a muffin tin. With your thumb make indentation in top of each brioche and fill with 1-inch marbles made from remaining dough. Slip muffin tins into large plastic bag and refrigerate overnight.* The next morning remove brioche from refrigerator and let stand in a warm place about 15 minutes.

Final Preparation When ready to bake, combine 1 egg yolk with 1 teaspoon water. Use to brush top of each brioche. Bake at 375 degrees 15 minutes.

1 egg yolk
1 teaspoon water

*Cook's Tip: To bake brioche on same day: after shaping, cover with towel and allow to rise in a warm place for 1 hour. Brush with egg glaze. Bake at 375 degrees for 15 minutes.

Little Jars of Jam

Transfer to jam pots or old-fashioned fruit jars, a selection of the best imported jams you can find. Other containers you might use are pots-de-crèmes or individual soufflé dishes.

3 jars of jam, assorted flavors

Pineapple Cooler
Croque Monsieur   *Scalloped Apples*
Holiday Cookie Assortment
Coffee with Cognac Chantilly

This menu was originally designed for a series of holiday lessons. Girls who were attending my classes at the time asked for a very special menu for Christmas morning that could be done ahead so they could relax while opening presents with their children. And yet they wanted it to be festive enough for the occasion.

When I suggested a grilled ham and cheese sandwich, there was an awkward silence until I added, "the delicious French one, Croque Monsieur." Many hostesses were delighted with this menu and it has proven to be a success at other festive family celebrations, including birthday parties and graduations.

Practically everything on this menu can be partially prepared ahead and held overnight. The next morning you can serve the pineapple cooler as an eye-opener while baking the apples. Fifteen minutes before moving your family or guests to the dining room, you can slip into the kitchen to finish the sandwiches.

At holiday time, many women have taken to "international-cookie-baking" with all the energy and fervor one would expect to apply to a favorite sport. I am including recipes for three excellent European cookies which are easy to make and can be counted on for authenticity. They are sure to become family traditions.

In this menu, I am suggesting that you serve your holiday cookie assortment with coffee and Cognac Chantilly. I further suggest that at holiday time you omit a lot of dessert cookery *per se*. Instead, use all the wonderful goodies that are around anyway. After all, most holiday cookies and sweetmeats represent the maker's greatest culinary efforts and deserve a place in the menu rather than being "tasted up" at odd hours.

Pineapple Cooler

Mix the juice of 2 lemons and 1/3 cup sugar into one 46-ounce can pineapple juice. Chill until needed. At serving time, pour over ice cubes in old fashioned glass and garnish with wedge of fresh pineapple on skewer.

2 lemons
1/3 cup sugar
1 can (46-ounce) pineapple juice
1 fresh pineapple, peeled, cored and cut into wedges
1 package 5-inch skewers

Croque Monsieur (Grilled Ham and Cheese Sandwich)

Advance Preparation Allow 2 slices sandwich bread per person. Trim crusts and spread with soft butter. Place one thin slice each Swiss cheese and ham on buttered side of bread. (May be wrapped in waxed paper and held overnight.)

16 slices sandwich bread
¼ cup softened butter
8 slices Swiss cheese
8 thin slices ham

Final Preparation Beat together 3 eggs and ¾ cup milk. Heat butter in a 15-inch electric frypan. Dip each sandwich into egg mixture and grill in butter over moderate heat until nicely browned. By cooking it slowly, the interior of the sandwich is cooked before the exterior gets too brown. Transfer to heated serving platter. May be kept in warm oven up to 30 minutes.

3 eggs
¾ cup milk
¼ cup butter

Scalloped Apples

Advance Preparation (1) Pare 6 to 8 tart cooking apples. Quarter, remove cores and cut into ¼-inch slices. Toss with 2 tablespoons lemon juice.
(2) Dissolve 2 tablespoons cornstarch in ¼ cup apple cider.* Combine with

6 to 8 cooking apples
2 tablespoon lemon juice

½ cup each sugar and apricot jam. Stir into apples to coat them evenly. (3) Place in buttered baking dish, cover and refrigerate overnight.
Final Preparation Bake apples, covered, at 350 degrees for 40 minutes. (Bake 30 minutes if not refrigerated.) Top each serving with a spoonful of dairy sour cream.

*Cook's Tip: For apple cider, you may substitute either apple wine or apple juice. The idea is to look for ways to reinforce flavors with *like* flavors, and avoid cooking with water whenever you have a reasonable choice.

2 tablespoons cornstarch
¼ cup apple cider
½ cup sugar
½ cup apricot jam

Swedish Butter Balls

(1) Cream together ½ cup butter and 2 tablespoons sugar. Add 1 teaspoon vanilla, a pinch of salt, 1 cup sifted all-purpose flour, and 1 cup ground pecans. (Pecans may be ground in blender to consistency of corn meal.)
(2) Shape dough into just smaller than 1-inch balls and place on ungreased baking sheet. Bake at 400 degrees about 10 minutes or until pale golden. Remove to paper towels. Roll in confectioners' sugar. Repeat if necessary to coat evenly.

½ cup butter
2 tablespoons sugar
1 teaspoon vanilla
Pinch salt
1 cup all-purpose flour
1 cup ground pecans
Confectioners' sugar

Berliner Kransers, Ragna Oas (Berlin Wreaths)

(1) Work 4 hard-cooked egg yolks

into 1 cup sifted all-purpose flour by hand until crumbly.

(2) In large mixer bowl, cream together one pound unsalted butter* and ¼ cup granulated sugar. Add flour and egg yolk mixture and continue beating. Add 2 more cups of flour and beat until well combined. Work in remaining cup of flour by hand. Wrap in waxed paper and chill overnight.

(3) With a knife cut off pieces of dough and roll into 5-inch lengths the size of a pencil. Pull the ends together and cross over, pressing together at point of overlap. Brush with beaten egg white. Dip in pearl or granulated sugar. Place on lightly oiled baking sheet. Bake at 350 degrees for 10 to 12 minutes or until golden.

*COOK'S TIP: If unsalted butter is not available, place 1 pound salted butter in large mixing bowl. Add 1 cup cold water and work it through the butter. Discard the water and repeat process. Use butter as usual.

4 hard-cooked egg yolks
4 cups all-purpose flour
1 pound unsalted butter
¼ cup granulated sugar
1 egg white, beaten
¼ cup pearl or granulated sugar

Almond Macaroons

Cut up 8 ounces almond paste and place in small mixer bowl. Add 1 cup sugar and 2 egg whites. Beat until smooth and fluffy. Using two teaspoons, make 1-inch mounds of mixture on an oiled baking sheet. Flatten each mound slightly with the back of a spoon. Bake at 325 degrees for 30 minutes. While warm, remove from

1 can (8-ounce) almond paste
1 cup sugar
2 egg whites

pan with spatula. Cool and store in sealed jars.

Cook's Tip: Most European dessert recipes that call for macaroons are referring to Almond Macaroons.

Cognac Chantilly (Cognac Whipped Cream)

Place 1 cup well-chilled whipping cream in small mixer bowl. Beat until cream begins to thicken. Add 3 tablespoons confectioners' sugar, one tablespoon at a time. Cease beating when soft peaks form. Stir in 1 tablespoon Cognac.
Service Place Cognac Chantilly in a small pitcher with a ladle. Pass as a topping for the second cup of coffee.

1 cup whipping cream
3 tablespoons confectioners' sugar
1 tablespoon Cognac

Chambraise on the Rocks
Sherried Ham and Turkey in Patty Shells
French-Style Green Peas   Lemon-Glazed Carrots
Sour Cream Coffee Cake
Coffee

Brunch time entertaining works out well before afternoon sporting events, and also for holiday parties when guests just can't face another huge sit-down dinner. This menu features foods which lend themselves well to buffet service. And this in turn allows for expanding the guest list.

As an apértif you might enjoy serving Chambraise, a light and delicate vermouth, flavored with wild strawberries. Whole, fresh strawberries make a delectable and succulent garnish, reinforcing the strawberry flavor of the wine which can be served on the rocks.

In this menu we make Sauce Béchamel for the first time and learn that this basic French white sauce differs from America's basic white sauce only in the seasoning. The method is the same. This version contains shallots, white pepper, and nutmeg. You will find that I use Sauce Béchamel as a base for soufflés and also for Sauce Mornay. Actually, it is a "mother sauce" and the possible variations are endless. In this menu, cubes of ham, turkey and sautéed sliced mushrooms are added to the basic sauce. A final dash of sherry is added to make a delectable filling for patty shells.

Patty shells come into their own when served for brunch. They can be attractively served from a napkin-lined basket, and each guest may fill his own shell from a chafing dish. Glazed baby carrots and little French peas complement this entrée nicely. They can be colorfully presented in a double candle-warmer serving dish.

This menu is planned for eight people. However, it is easy to expand. Should you decide to use it for a large party, you might enjoy serving dessert and coffee from a location other than the main buffet. This coffee cake is so attractive that you might want to make two of them. Place one on a pedestal cake stand to be enjoyed for its handsome appearance, and slice one to serve. Don't worry; the second cake won't last long

Chambraise on the Rocks
(Vermouth Apéritif)

Fill 8 old fashioned glasses with ice cubes and half-fill glasses with Chambraise. Spear a whole fresh strawberry and a sprig of mint on a cocktail skewer and use as garnish.

1 pint strawberries
1 sprig mint per serving
1 bottle Chambraise

Sherried Ham and Turkey

Advance Preparation (1) *S a u c e*

1 shallot

Béchamel Sauté one minced shallot in 4 tablespoons butter until translucent. Stir in 4 tablespoons flour and cook one minute without browning. Add 2 cups milk and stir steadily with a wire whisk. Add 1 teaspoon salt, a pinch of white pepper and a grating of nutmeg. Continue whisking until thickened and keep warm over hot water.

(2) *Ham* Cut about 1½ pounds ready-to-eat ham into ½-inch cubes. Sauté briefly in 2 tablespoons butter until lightly browned. Remove from heat and drizzle with 2 tablespoons sherry. Stir into sauce.

(3) *Turkey* From a pre-roasted, rolled turkey roast or leftover turkey, cut ½-inch cubes to equal 1½ cups. Stir into sauce with ham.

(4) *Mushrooms* Wash, trim and slice ½ pound mushrooms from stem through cap. Sauté until lightly browned in 2 tablespoons butter. Stir into ham and turkey.

Final Preparation Transfer to chafing dish and keep over hot water until serving time. Add 2 tablespoons more sherry and a small cube of butter before serving. (Sauce will be sufficient to fill 4 additional patty shells, if second servings are desired.)

4 tablespoons butter
4 tablespoons flour
2 cups milk
1 teaspoon salt
Pinch white pepper (1/8 teaspoon)
A grating fresh nutmeg (1/8 teaspoon)

1½ pounds ready-to-eat ham
2 tablespoons butter
1½ pounds pre-cooked turkey
4 tablespoons dry sherry
½ pound mushrooms
2 tablespoons butter

Patty Shells

Prepare 8 frozen patty shells according to package directions.

8 frozen patty shells

French-Style Green Peas

(1) Place 2 packages partially thawed frozen tiny green peas in skillet. Add 2 sliced green onions, one sprig minced parsley, 1 teaspoon salt, and 2 tablespoons butter. Shred ¼ head iceberg lettuce and distribute evenly over peas.* (Set aside until about 8 minutes before serving time.)

(2) Turn on heat and simmer peas gently under their lettuce cover about 4 minutes. Stir in lettuce, turning peas to come in contact with heat evenly, and continue cooking about 2 minutes. Stir in 1 tablespoon additional butter and toss until glazed.

*Variation: Omit shredded lettuce. Instead, cook the peas under a whole lettuce leaf, which is discarded. During the last one minute of cooking, add ¼ pound fresh pea pods.

2 packages (10-ounce) frozen tiny peas
2 green onions, sliced
1 sprig parsley, minced
1 teaspoon salt
2 tablespoons butter
¼ head lettuce, shredded
1 tablespoon butter

Lemon-Glazed Carrots

Advance Preparation (1) Peel 2 pounds carrots. Cut into 1½-inch uniform lengths, and carve each end to resemble baby carrots. (Or cut on the oblique into rounds with a crinkle cutter.) Drop into boiling salted water and simmer, covered, for 15 minutes or until tender. Drain and reserve until just prior to serving.

2 pounds slender carrots
Boiling salted water, to cover

Final Preparation Combine in a skillet 4 tablespoons butter, 1 tablespoon sugar, the grated rind of one lemon,

4 tablespoons butter
1 tablespoon sugar
Grated rind of one lemon

and 1 tablespoon lemon juice. Heat the mixture and add the carrots. Shake skillet, tossing carrots gently until they are heated through and well glazed.

1 tablespoon lemon juice

Sour Cream Coffee Cake

(1) *Cake Batter* Cream together in large mixer bowl 1 cup butter and 1¼ cups granulated sugar. Add 2 eggs one at a time, beating well after each addition. Add 1 cup dairy sour cream and 1 teaspoon vanilla. Sift together 2 cups all-purpose flour, 1 teaspoon salt, ½ teaspoon soda and 1½ teaspoons baking powder. Beat into creamed mixture.

1 cup butter
1¼ cups granulated sugar
2 eggs
1 cup dairy sour cream
1 teaspoon vanilla
2 cups all-purpose flour
1 teaspoon salt
½ teaspoon soda
1½ teaspoons baking powder

(2) *Filling* Combine ½ cup chopped walnuts, ¼ cup brown sugar and 1 teaspoon cinnamon.

½ cup chopped walnuts
¼ cup brown sugar
1 teaspoon cinnamon

(3) Butter and flour a 9-inch tube pan. Spoon half of the filling into bottom of pan. Add half of the cake batter and sprinkle with remaining filling. Add remainder of cake batter. Pick the pan up and jolt the bottom flatly against the counter to settle batter evenly. Bake at 350 degrees for 45 to 50 minutes. Cool 10 to 15 minutes before inverting pan.

(4) *Service* Place on cake stand and dust lightly with confectioners' sugar. Slice and serve with Cognac Chantilly.

1 to 2 tablespoons confectioners' sugar

1 recipe Cognac Chantilly (Page 9)

Iced Tomato Juice Cocktail
Eggs Benedict with Extra English Muffins
Prunes à la Alice B. Toklas
or
Oranges Grand Marnier
Coffee

There are lots of eager cooks around these days who are creative and adventurous. They don't hesitate to tackle new techniques that come along. But what about the old techniques? If you ever went before a board of examiners for an evaluation of your cooking skills, chances are the very first thing you'd be asked to make would be Eggs Benedict.

Among the old skills, you might find yourself attempting to poach a lot of eggs at one time. The classic method of doing this is included in this menu, and you'll find that it is really very easy. (On the other hand, if the manual approach baffles you in any way, don't hesitate to acquire some of the new equipment designed for poaching eggs.)

Hollandaise sauce, whether made by the old hand-beating method or the newer blender approach, still relies on a lot of action to incorporate all those egg yolks into the butter. There is little doubt that the blender method produces a more stable sauce. Certainly the blender method takes a lot of anxiety out of the procedure, and you can count on a successful sauce the very first time you try it. Someday when there is no pressure on you, whip out your blender and run through this recipe. The most you have to lose by a test run is about 75 cents, which is a small price to pay for learning such a valuable technique.

Although Eggs Benedict are not limited seasonally, other foods for this menu can be selected with seasonal considerations in mind. During winter months you might enjoy a winter fruit, such as prunes cooked in the style of Alice B. Toklas. Such a sumptuous dish! Just a few prunes are cooked in a whole bottle of Port.* In summer months you might switch to Oranges Grand Marnier, just as elegant but their color and flavor are better suited to the mood of a warm sunny morning.

Until you have mastered the technique of making Eggs Benedict, you'd be well advised to limit the guest list to no more than eight.

*Cook's Tip: If you choose to serve Prunes à la Alice B. Toklas, remember to begin their preparation at least five days before your party.

Iced Tomato Juice Cocktail

(1) Combine in top of blender 1 green onion, sprig parsley, ½ rib chopped celery, ½ peeled chopped cucumber, 1 teaspoon horseradish, the juice of 1 lemon and 1 cup tomato juice from a 46-ounce can. Blend until smooth. Pour remaining tomato juice into a pitcher and stir in contents of blender. Chill until needed.
(2) At serving time pour over ice cubes in old fashioned glasses.

1 green onion
1 sprig parsley
½ rib celery, chopped
½ cucumber, peeled and chopped
1 teaspoon horseradish
Juice of 1 lemon (3 to 4 tablespoons)
1 can (46-ounce) tomato juice

Eggs Benedict

Advance Preparation (1) *Hollandaise Sauce* Combine in warmed blender container 2 tablespoons lemon juice, 4 egg yolks, ¼ teaspoon paprika and ½ teaspoon salt. Heat 1 cup butter until completely melted, without stirring. Skim off foam and pour clear butter into another saucepan, leaving milk solids behind. (This is then clarified butter.) Add 3 tablespoons boiling water to the clarified butter and heat briefly. Turn on blender and begin pouring hot butter in a slow steady stream into natural whirlpool formed by spinning blades of blender.

2 tablespoons lemon juice
4 egg yolks
¼ teaspoon paprika
½ teaspoon salt
1 cup clarified butter
3 tablespoons boiling water

When sauce has thickened and butter is incorporated, cease blending. Place entire container, covered, in warm water until serving time.

(2) Split English muffins and spread lightly with butter. Place on baking sheet and toast in a 375-degree oven for 10 to 12 minutes, or until lightly browned. Sauté one slice of ham or Canadian bacon for each serving. Top toasted muffins with ham and place on a heated serving platter. Keep in warm oven.

6 English muffins, split
4 tablespoons soft butter
12 slices ham or Canadian bacon

(3) *Poached Eggs* Fill a 12 or 15-inch skillet 2 inches deep with water. Add ½ teaspoon salt and 1 tablespoon vinegar to each quart of water. Bring to a boil and reduce heat to simmer. Break each egg directly into water. With a spoon, gently push the whites toward the yolks to shape. As soon as each egg has taken on a solid appearance (about 4 minutes) remove it with a slotted spoon. Plunge immediately into cold water. Hold until needed.

½ teaspoon salt and 1 tablespoon vinegar per quart water
12 eggs

Final Preparation At serving time, trim away any ragged edges with a sharp knife. Place eggs in small amount of salted water and bring to a boil. Leave eggs only until heated through. Remove eggs with a slotted spoon and place them on prepared English muffins topped with ham. Spoon generous amounts of Hollandaise over each. If you have been saving a can of truffles for a special occasion, the time has arrived. Cut them

1 can (7/8-ounce) truffles, optional

into uniform 1/16-inch dice and use to garnish each serving of Eggs Benedict.

Prunes à la Alice B. Toklas

Advance Preparation (1) Five days before needed, place 1½ pounds large pitted prunes in enameled vessel and add 1 fifth California port wine. Let stand 24 hours.
(2) Add 1 cup sugar and place on heat. Simmer 30 minutes. Cool and refrigerate 3 days.
Final Preparation Place prunes in attractive serving dish. Cover with 1 cup slightly sweetened whipped cream. Crush 3 almond macaroons and scatter on top. Stud surface with crystalized violets. (Available in gourmet food and specialty shops.)

1½ pounds large pitted prunes
1 fifth California port wine
1 cup sugar

1 cup whipping cream, whipped and slightly sweetened
3 almond macaroons (Page 8)
6 to 8 crystallized violets

Oranges Grand Marnier

Advance Preparation (1) Select 8 small navel oranges, 2 to 3 inches across. Remove zest (just the orange textured surface of the skin) with a vegetable peeler. Cut the zest of two oranges into matchstick strips and blanch 3 minutes in boiling water.
(2) Drain the strips and place in a saucepan with 1 cup water and 3 cups sugar. Simmer about 10 minutes. Remove from heat and cool. Add ¼ cup Grand Marnier.*
(3) While the syrup is cooling, completely remove the remaining white pulp from the surfaces of the oranges

8 small navel oranges
1 cup water
3 cups sugar
¼ cup Grand Marnier

and leave whole. Place oranges in container and add the syrup. Refrigerate overnight.

Final Preparation Transfer oranges to individual dessert dishes. Spoon on generous amounts of sauce and candied orange peel. Provide fruit knives for guests.

*Cook's Tip: For Grand Marnier, you may substitute any of the orange-flavored liqueurs such as Cointreau, Triple-Sec or Curaçao. If you don't have any of these on hand use the grand old standby of dessert cookery, Kirsch. And if you don't have Kirsch, go out and buy some.

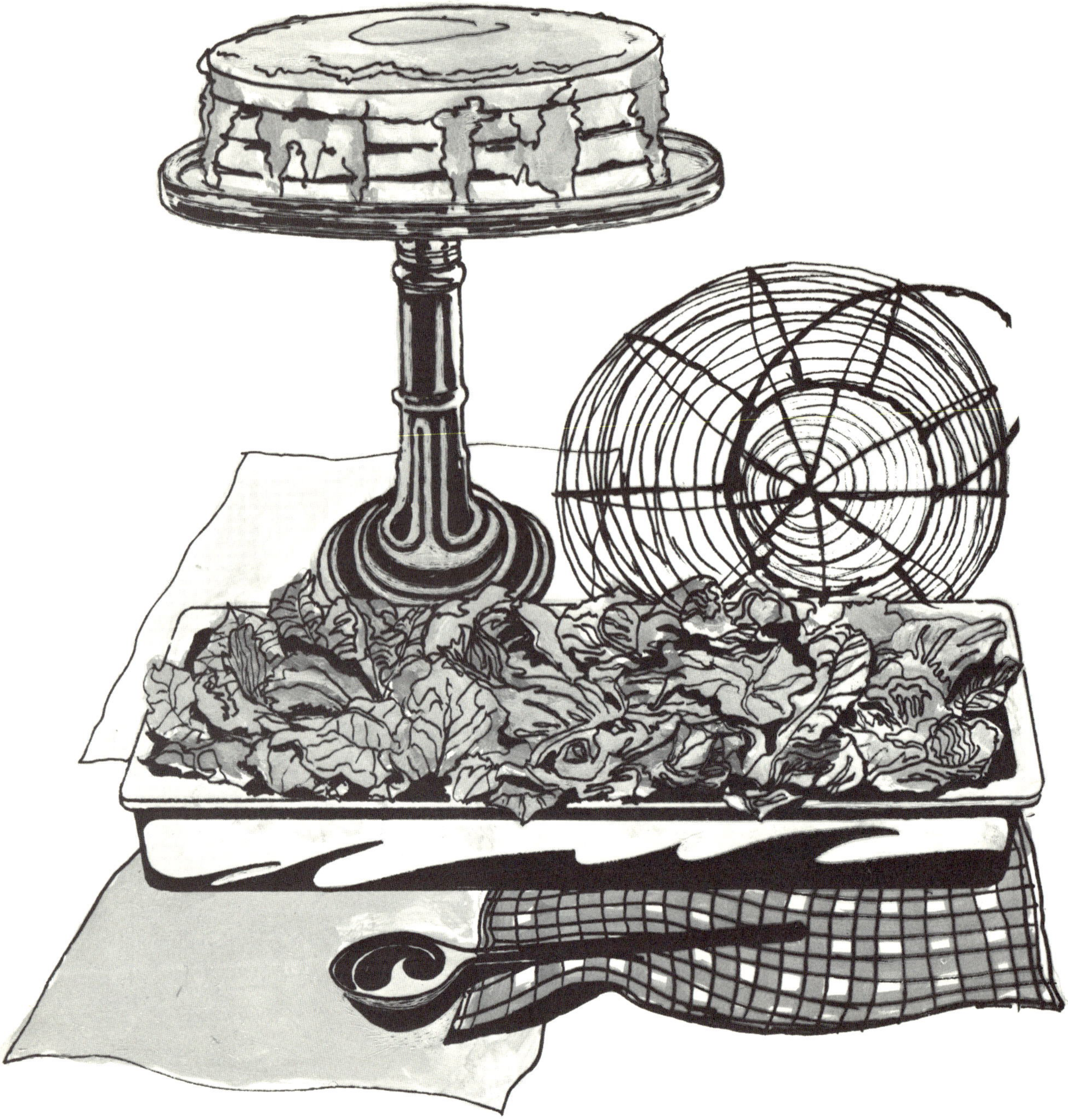

II SALAD-PLUS MENUS

Big hearty salads plus one complementary dish and dessert. These menus are for casual buffet service which allows guests to move around a little and exercise options as to caloric intake.

Quiche Lorraine   Salade Nicoise
Gateau du Jour

With the Quiche,
Johannisberger Riesling

As soon as the word gets out that you like to cook, someone is sure to give you a quiche dish . . . lucky you! Just so you won't have to scrounge around for good recipes, I am giving you two. One is "from scratch" with a fine homemade crust which I hope you will commit to memory. The other is a hurry-up version for busy days which is just about as good. Either one is a good beginning for this salad-plus menu.

One of the most loved of the big French salads is Salade Niçoise (Nee-swaz). Combination salads such as this, which are generously endowed with lots of interesting ingredients, are entirely suitable to be served as an entrée. While touring

Nice and environs, I ordered Salade Niçoise every day for a week, and each time it was a greater delight than the day before. Of course, there were variations of ingredients according to the fancy of the cook, but all of the salads contained tuna, ripe olives and lots of tomatoes. The dressings were crisp, tangy and subtly flavored with herbs. Most of them contained less greenery than our American adaptations, but the flavors in the one included here were much the same.

There is little technique involved in producing a successful old-fashioned two-egg layer cake, which for the sake of continuity I am calling Gateau du Jour. About the only mistake you can make is overbeating. After combining the ingredients beat only until blended. This cake is as handy as a mix, and especially good when served fresh and slightly warm.

Quiche Lorraine (Savory Cheese Tarte)

(1) *Basic Pie Crust* Into a bowl sift and measure 1¼ cups all-purpose flour and ¼ teaspoon salt. Add 2 tablespoons butter and 1/3 cup vegetable shortening. Cut shortening into flour with a pastry blender. Cease cutting when fat particles remain as large as small peas. Gradually sprinkle 3 to 4 tablespoons ice water over mixture and stir with a fork until dough begins to hold together. Shape pastry into a ball by hand.

(2) On a floured board roll pie crust into a circle just larger than your pie pan or quiche dish. Fit into pan and trim away excess pastry. Line the crust with waxed paper and fill with dry beans.* Bake at 400 degrees for

1¼ cups all-purpose flour
¼ teaspoon salt
2 tablespoons butter
1/3 cup vegetable shortening
3 to 4 tablespoons ice water

Strip of waxed paper
*1 pound dry uncooked beans**

12 minutes. Remove beans and paper and return to oven for another 5 minutes. Reserve.

(3) *Cheese, Ham and Custard* Sauté together in 2 tablespoons butter, 1 thinly sliced yellow onion and 1 cup finely diced ham. Distribute evenly over bottom of crust. Top with 1 cup shredded Swiss cheese. Beat together 2 eggs, 1 cup evaporated milk, ⅛ teaspoon white pepper and ½ teaspoon each salt, dry mustard, and paprika. Pour mixture over contents of shell. Bake at 375 degrees for 35 minutes or until set. Cool slightly before cutting in wedges to serve.

*Cook's Tip: Beans are used to keep the crust flat and are not harmed by heat once or twice. They can be cooked as usual, or reserved just for pie crust.

2 tablespoons butter
1 yellow onion, thinly sliced
1 cup finely diced ham
1 cup shredded Swiss cheese
2 eggs
1 cup evaporated milk
1/8 teaspoon white pepper
½ teaspoon salt
½ teaspoon dry mustard
½ teaspoon paprika

Alternate Quick Quiche

(1) Line pie pan or buttered quiche dish with one can refrigerated crescent dinner rolls. Just pat them in to fit pan, pressing seams together.

(2) Fry 9 strips bacon and crumble into bottom of shell. Top with 1 cup shredded Swiss cheese, and one can French fried onion rings.

(3) Beat together 1 egg, 1 cup evaporated milk, ½ teaspoon salt, and 1 teaspoon Worcestershire sauce. Pour over contents of shell. Bake at 375 degrees for 35 minutes or until set.

1 can refrigerated crescent dinner rolls

9 strips bacon
1 cup shredded Swiss cheese
1 can (3-ounce) French fried onion rings

1 egg
1 cup evaporated milk
½ teaspoon salt
1 teaspoon Worcestershire sauce

COOK'S TIP: Evaporated milk is recommended for both of these recipes, as it helps to insure a crisp crust.

Salade Niçoise (Salad in the style of Nice)

Advance Preparation (1) Remove bruised and unsound outer leaves from one head each iceberg lettuce and romaine. Wash in cold water and shake dry in a salad basket. Roll in a large kitchen towel and refrigerate until needed.

1 head iceberg lettuce
1 head romaine

(2) *Sauce Vinaigrette aux Fines Herbes* Combine in a screw-top jar ¼ cup white wine vinegar, 1 teaspoon salt, and a little freshly ground black pepper. Add ½ teaspoon each tarragon and chervil. Add 1 sprig finely minced parsley and either freshly snipped chives or 1 teaspoon freeze-dried chives. As soon as the salt has dissolved and the dried herbs have freshened, add ¾ cup salad oil and shake. The salad oil may be partially olive oil, for flavor variation.

¼ cup white wine vinegar
1 teaspoon salt
Freshly ground black pepper
½ teaspoon tarragon
½ teaspoon chervil
Sprig minced parsley
1 teaspoon chives
¾ cup salad oil (may be part olive oil)

(3) *Green Beans Vinaigrette* Place 2 tablespoons water in a skillet and add 1 package partially thawed whole green beans. Cook uncovered 4 to 5 minutes, or until tender, but remaining just slightly crisp to the bite, "al dente." Toss hot beans with 2 tablespoons Sauce Vinaigrette, and sprinkle with salt to taste. Chill and drain before adding to salad.

2 tablespoons water
1 package (9-ounce) frozen whole green beans
2 tablespoons Sauce Vinaigrette
Salt to taste

(4) *French Potato Salad* Drain 1 can sliced potatoes and rinse under cool running water. Dissolve 1 teaspoon instant chicken bouillon in ¼ cup water in a large skillet. Add the potatoes and cook over high heat, shaking pan until all bouillon is absorbed. Toss potatoes while still hot with 3 tablespoons Sauce Vinaigrette and add 1 tablespoon each finely minced green onion and parsley.

1 can (1-pound) sliced potatoes
1 teaspoon instant chicken bouillon
¼ cup water
3 tablespoons Sauce Vinaigrette
1 tablespoon minced parsley
1 tablespoon minced green onion

(5) *Hard-Cooked Eggs* Place 4 eggs in cold water to cover. In order to keep yolks centered, keep them moving around until water comes to a boil. Reduce heat to simmer and continue cooking 12 minutes. (Do use a timer for this.) Drain off hot water and cover eggs with cold water immediately. Any number of eggs may be cooked in this way.

4 eggs
Cold water to cover

(6) *Other Additions* One can each albacore tuna, pitted ripe olives, and rolled anchovies, opened and drained. One red onion, sliced. Two tablespoons each finely minced parsley and green onion. Three or four ripe tomatoes, cut into wedges and sprinkled with salt.

1 can (7-ounce) albacore tuna
1 can (7½-ounce) pitted ripe olives
1 flat tin rolled anchovies
1 red onion, sliced
2 tablespoons minced parsley
2 tablespoons minced green onion
3 or 4 tomatoes, cut into wedges

Final Preparation Break prepared greens into a chilled salad bowl and toss with just enough Sauce Vinaigrette to make greens glisten. Taste, and add salt and pepper if necessary. Add tuna, pitted ripe olives, red onion rings, green beans and potato salad, and roll these gently into greens. Pull more interesting items to the surface and arrange the rolled anchovies, quartered eggs, and sliced tomatoes on top. Garnish with minced parsley and green onion. Serve at once.

Gateau du Jour (Everyday Jam Cake)

(1) *Cake Batter* Cream together in large mixer bowl ½ cup butter, 1 cup sugar and 1 teaspoon vanilla. Add 2 eggs and beat until blended.
(2) Sift and measure 2 cups all-purpose flour. Combine with 1 tablespoon baking powder and ½ teaspoon salt. Add to creamed mixture with 1 cup whole milk. Beat only until blended.
(3) Lightly oil a 9" layer cake pan with 2" sides. Dust with flour. Cut waxed paper to fit bottom of pan and place over flour. Spoon in the cake batter and bake at 350 degrees for 30 minutes. Cool in pan on a rack.
(4) *Filling* As soon as cake is cool enough to handle, invert it onto your hand and quickly peel off the waxed paper. Place cake smooth-side-up on serving dish. Split in half and spread ¾ cup apricot jam* between layers.
(5) *Decoration and Service* Place a lace paper doily on top of cake. Sift 2 to 3 tablespoons confectioners' sugar evenly over top. Carefully remove doily. Serve the cake warm, or at room temperature.
Variation To suit your flavor fancy, on other occasions use cherry, strawberry, blueberry or raspberry jam.

½ cup butter
1 cup sugar
1 teaspoon vanilla
2 eggs

2 cups all-purpose flour
1 tablespoon baking powder
½ teaspoon salt
1 cup whole milk

Waxed paper for lining

¾ cup apricot jam

2 to 3 tablespoons confectioners' sugar

Raclette
Boiled Potatoes   *Cornichons*   *Pickled Onions*
Chef's Salad Bar
Chocolate Raspberry Torte

With the Raclette, Fendant or Neuchâtel

For those who ski and participate in other winter sports, here is a salad-plus Raclette menu for an informal gathering. It offers a pleasant change from that old standby, cheese fondue, and it requires none of the skill and/or luck that it takes to produce a successful fondue.

I first enjoyed Raclette in Zermatt, Switzerland. Immediately upon my return I set out to duplicate this melted cheese specialty.

In days gone by, Raclette was made by placing a half wheel of cheese near a wood-burning fire, and as the surface layer of cheese melted it was scraped onto the plates of eagerly waiting guests. With the advent of electricity, the innovative Swiss were quick to engineer a special "raclette stove." It is a wrought-iron rack which holds a half wheel of cheese under an electric broiler for the melting process.

Lacking both the patience required for melting the cheese by a wood-burning fire, and not possessing a "raclette stove," I fabricated my own method of preparing Raclette. I place several layers of thinly sliced raclette cheese (for raclette cheese, any good fondue cheese such as Fontina, Monterrey Jack, or Swiss can be substituted) in individual "au gratin" dishes and slip them into a 400-degree oven until the cheese has melted. The hot "au gratin" dishes are transferred to service plates. The melted cheese is traditionally eaten with little potatoes boiled in their jackets, tiny dilled pickles (cornichons) and cocktail onions. It may tax the imagination to say that these humble foods when served together, somehow border on greatness. But once you've tried it, I am sure you will agree that they do.

The entrée salad selected for this menu is an adaptation of the plentifully supplied salad bars which are found in Rocky Mountain ski areas. A large bowl of assorted salad greens, plus those ingredients usually found in a Chef's salad, are provided. Guests may help themselves as the spirit moves them.

In contrast to these simple foods, you will enjoy serving this regal Chocolate Raspberry Torte which is adapted from another specialty found in Zermatt. Crowned with whipped cream and crystalized violets, it goes well with black coffee.

When you say goodnight to those who must rise early and get back on the slopes, it will be no secret that your status as a hostess has gained a few points.

Racelette (Melted Cheese à la Suisse

(1) *Potatoes* You will need 2 to 4 small uniform white or new potatoes per person. Scrub them leaving the skins intact, and drop into boiling salted water. Cook covered 25 minutes or until tender. Drain and place in a napkin-lined silver bowl.

16 to 32 small potatoes
Salted water to cover

(2) *Cornichons and Onions* Combine 1 pint tiny dilled gherkins and ½ pint cocktail onions. Place in an earthy-looking crock.

1 pint tiny dilled gherkins
½ pint cocktail onions

(3) *The Cheese* Slice 2 pounds raclette (or a good quality fondue-type) cheese into thin slices and layer into eight 6-inch au gratin dishes. Ten minutes prior to serving time, place in a 400-degree oven. Bake 10 minutes.

2 pounds raclette cheese, Fontina, Monterrey Jack or Swiss

(4) *Service* Provide one large, easy-to-handle dinner plate per guest. Transfer Raclette in hot au gratin dishes to dinner plates and deliver to guests. (Husband or another guest may help.)

Place potatoes, pepper grinders, pickles and onions in convenient locations for self service, or pass on a tray. Guests spear potatoes and cut them into pieces on their plates. They are sprinkled with a little freshly ground black pepper and each piece of potato is swirled in melted cheese. It is eaten alternately with pickles and onions.

COOK'S TIP: If you plan to have seconds (in Switzerland seconds are expected, even thirds), place a platter of pre-sliced cheese with instructions near the oven, where guests may help themselves.

Organization of the Chef's Salad Bar

(1) Select 2 or more salad greens from the checklist (opposite), sufficient to make 4 quarts broken greens. You might choose 2 heads red or green leaf lettuce, 1 romaine and 1 iceberg.

(2) Remove bruised and unsound outer leaves and separate inner leaves. Wash in large amounts of cold water. Swing in a salad basket to remove excess water. Roll in kitchen towels and refrigerate until serving time. At serving time break the leaves into large bite sizes, discarding hard cores and place in chilled salad bowl. Sprinkle with generous amounts of finely minced parsley. Place on buffet table where guests may conveniently help themselves.

(3) *Preparation of Salad Additions*

Checklist for Salad Greens:
Iceberg
Boston or Bibb
Red or green leaf lettuce
Romaine
Escarole
Belgium endive
Curly endive
Chicory
Spinach
Watercress

1 bunch parsley, finely minced

4 poached breasts of chicken

Arrange a selection of meats and condiments from which guests may choose, using low, flat dishes of uniform size. Failing all else, pyrex from the hardware will do. It is the symmetry and repetition that make this bar attractive. Fill each dish with one of the following: sliced breast of cold chicken, slivered ready-to-eat ham, matchsticks of Swiss cheese, quartered hard-cooked eggs, mixed ripe and green olives, quartered tomatoes, red onions, sliced into rings, and croutons.

1 pound ready-to-eat ham
1 pound Swiss cheese
6 hard-cooked eggs
1 can (7½-ounce) ripe olives
1 can (7½-ounce) green olives
6 tomatoes, quartered
2 red onions, sliced
1 box (7-ounce) seasoned salad croutons

A Trio of Great Salad Dressings
Blender Vinaigrette à la Moutarde (French Dressing with Mustard)

Place in top of blender: ¼ cup white wine vinegar, 1 teaspoon salt, a little freshly ground black pepper, and ½ teaspoon each tarragon, chervil, and Dijon mustard. Add 1 chopped green onion, ¼ cup olive oil and 1 whole fresh egg. Blend a few seconds and add 1 cup safflower oil in a slow steady stream, as blender continues to run.

¼ cup white wine vinegar
1 teaspoon salt
Freshly ground black pepper
½ teaspoon tarragon
½ teaspoon chervil
½ teaspoon Dijon mustard
1 green onion, chopped
¼ cup olive oil
1 whole egg
1 cup safflower oil

Green Goddess

In bowl, combine 3 tablespoons each tarragon wine vinegar and lemon juice. Add 1 clove pressed garlic, 2 tablespoons anchovy paste and ¼ cup finely minced parsley. Stir in 1 cup mayonnaise and 1 cup dairy sour cream.

3 tablespoons tarragon wine vinegar
3 tablespoons lemon juice
1 clove garlic, pressed
2 tablspoons anchovy paste
¼ cup minced parsley
1 cup mayonnaise
1 cup dairy sour cream

Roquefort Sour Cream Dressing

Mix together ½ teaspoon each garlic salt, celery salt, paprika, and black pepper. Add 1 teaspoon salt and 2 tablespoons white wine vinegar. Blend in ½ cup mayonnaise and 1 cup dairy sour cream. Crumble and fold in 4 ounces Roquefort cheese.

COOK'S TIP: These dressings happen to be of similar color so place them in bowls of assorted colors.

½ teaspoon garlic salt
½ teaspoon celery salt
½ teaspoon paprika
½ teaspoon black pepper
1 teaspoon salt
2 tablespoons white wine vinegar
½ cup mayonnaise
1 cup dairy sour cream
4 ounces Roquefort cheese

Chocolate Raspberry Torte

COOK'S TIP: Be sure to make this cake up to Final Preparation, and refrigerate it overnight. The flavors need an opportunity to mellow. Frost with whipped cream just prior to service.

Advance Preparation (1) *Cake Batter* Combine in saucepan 1½ cups ground pecans or English walnuts, ¾ cup red Burgundy, 2 tablespoons fine bread crumbs, 6 ounces semi-sweet chocolate bits, and ¾ cup sugar. Cook over moderate heat, stirring constantly with a wire whisk until chocolate has melted and mixture begins to thicken. Remove from heat and cool.

(2) Separate 6 eggs. Beat the yolks until thick and lemon colored and fold into chocolate mixture.

(3) To the egg whites add ½ teaspoon cream of tartar and a pinch of salt. Beat the whites until stiff but not dry. Fold into chocolate mixture.

1½ cups ground pecans or English walnuts
¾ cup red Burgundy
2 tablespoons fine bread crumbs
6 ounces semi-sweet chocolate bits
¾ cup sugar

6 eggs, separated

½ teaspoon cream of tartar
Pinch of salt

(4) Place batter in 2 prepared 9-inch layer cake pans (To prepare pans, see Step 3 Page 26). Bake at 350 degrees for 30 minutes. Remove from oven, cool at least 10 minutes before removing from pans. Cool completely.
(5) Force 1½ cups raspberry jam through sieve to remove seeds. Add 1 tablespoon Framboise* or Kirsch and spread between the layers. (Preparation to this point should be done the day before.)

1½ cups raspberry jam
1 tablespoon Framboise* or Kirsch

Final Preparation Frost the top of cake with lightly sweetened whipped cream. Make a circle of whipped cream rosettes on top and place a crystallized violet on each rosette.

1 cup whipping cream, whipped and lightly sweetened
6 to 7 crystallized violets

*Cook's Tip: Framboise (fram-bwahz) is distilled raspberry brandy from France. It is also available in Germany where it is known as Himbeergeist. Look for it when traveling abroad. Whenever necessary, you may substitute Kirsch for Framboise.

French Onion Soup
Deluxe Salad California Style
Pineapple Upside-Down Cake Roll

With the Soup,
Amontillado Sherry, or Gewürtztraminer

Hardly any phase of cookery is as beset with "do's" and "don'ts" as salad making. The "don'ts" begin when you take a firm head of lettuce in hand and remember the ominous warning, "Don't ever cut salad greens with a knife!" Does this mean that we are to forego forever all the great things that happen with shredded lettuce, such as Celestial Salad in the Lotus Bowl Import menus, or this salad that we are about to make? There must be a reason for this emphatic proclamation. What could it be?

It could be that the carbon steel French knife, which is the workhorse of the kitchen and the revered accomplice of every good cook, has been misused for the delicate business of severing salad greens. Such a knife could have produced rust-tinged edges and possibly transmitted a metallic flavor to salad greens. So, when you have to shred greens as you do in Deluxe Salad California Style, "do" use a very sharp *stainless steel* knife.

This particular salad not only calls for shredded greenery but also for minced or diced salad additions as well. For this reason you are cautioned to delay the steps of final preparation until the very end. Your salad will look fresher and taste better if it is tossed with dressing just prior to service. Also, bear in mind when tossing the salad that the amount of vinaigrette used should be limited so that the ingredients just barely glisten with a thin coating of sauce.

Although Deluxe Salad California Style is an excellent salad for an entrée, it could be served in reverse order with the French Onion Soup. Either way, you are sure to like the Pineapple Upside-Down Cake Roll, which eliminates several steps of preparation by baking the filling right along with the cake. It is served topped with ginger-flavored whipped cream. Ginger provides a most fitting final flavor for this interesting Salad-Plus Menu which was inspired by travels in California.

French Onion Soup

(1) Sauté 2 to 3 pounds thinly sliced yellow onions in 2 tablespoons each butter and olive oil. Cover and cook over very low heat 15 to 20 minutes. Remove cover and add 1 teaspoon each sugar and salt. Stir until onions become golden. Stir in 3 to 4 table-

2 to 3 pounds yellow onions
2 tablespoons butter
2 tablespoons olive oil
1 teaspoon sugar
1 teaspoon salt
3 to 4 tablespoons flour
½ cup dry red or white wine

spoons flour. Add ½ cup dry red or white wine and 4 cans beef consommé plus two soup cans water. Add ½ teaspoon sage and 1 bay leaf. Simmer gently for 30 minutes. Remove bay leaf. Just before serving stir in 3 tablespoons brandy. Serve by either Service Method I or II below.

(2) Slice French bread into ½-inch slices and place on a baking sheet in a 325-degree oven for 15 minutes. Brush with olive oil and sprinkle with grated Parmesan or Romano cheese. Continue baking about 5 minutes.

SERVICE METHOD I Serve soup from tureen and ladle servings over toasted French bread in individual bowls. Have at hand grated Parmesan or Romano cheese to sprinkle on top.

SERVICE METHOD II Place soup in large flat oven-to-table casserole. Arrange the toasted French bread on top. Cover bread generously with ½ pound shredded Gruyère cheese and 2 tablespoons grated Parmesan or Romano. Place under broiler until cheese melts and browns lightly.

4 cans (10½-ounce) beef consommé
2 soup cans water
½ teaspoon sage
1 bay leaf
3 tablespoons brandy

1 slice French bread per serving
¼ cup olive oil
¼ cup grated Parmesan or Romano cheese

½ pound Gruyère cheese
2 tablespoons grated Parmesan or Romano cheese

Deluxe Salad California Style

Advance Preparation (1) Remove bruised and unsound outer leaves from one head each romaine, iceberg, and leaf lettuce. Wash in cold water, swing in salad basket to remove excess water, and roll into large kitchen towels. Refrigerate until time to assemble salad.

1 head romaine
1 head iceberg lettuce
1 head leaf lettuce

Cook's Tip: When preparing greens the night before, place towel filled with greenery inside large plastic bag.

(2) *Additions* Prepare and have ready: 2 cups finely cubed cooked breasts of chicken, 1 pound crumbled crisply fried bacon, 12 to 18 quartered cherry tomatoes, 1 can (14-ounce) artichoke hearts, 4 diced avocados (after avocados are diced toss them with juice of ½ lemon), 2 chopped hard-cooked eggs, and 2 tablespoons each finely minced parsley and green onion.

(3) Prepare one recipe Vinaigrette aux Fines Herbes, and one recipe Roquefort Sour Cream Dressing.

Final Preparation With a stainless steel knife, shred the prepared salad greens as finely as possible, discarding hard cores. Place in chilled salad bowl and add all ingredients from Step 2. Toss in a rolling motion with just enough Sauce Vinaigrette to make greens glisten. Taste and add salt and pepper if necessary. Place Roquefort Dressing in small pitcher with ladle so that guests may help themselves, as desired.

2 cups cubed breast of chicken
1 pound bacon, crisply fried
12 to 18 cherry tomatoes, quartered
1 can (14-ounce) artichoke hearts
4 avocados, diced
Juice of ½ lemon (1½ tablespoons)
2 hard-cooked eggs, chopped
2 tablespoons minced parsley
2 tablespoons minced green onion
1 recipe Vinaigrette (Page 24)
1 recipe Roquefort Sour Cream Dressing (Page 31)

Pineapple Upside-Down Cake Roll

(1) Melt ¼ cup butter. Stir in ¼ cup slivered almonds and ¾ cup brown sugar. When dissolved, add one can (20-ounce) crushed pineapple, well drained. Spread evenly in a 15" x 10" jelly roll pan.

¼ cup butter
¼ cup slivered almonds
¾ cup brown sugar
1 can (20-ounce) crushed pineapple, drained

(2) *Cake Batter* Beat 3 eggs well, slowly adding 1 cup granulated sugar. Add ¼ cup warm water and 1 teaspoon vanilla. Continue beating until thick and creamy. Combine 1 cup sifted all-purpose flour, 1 teaspoon baking powder and ¼ teaspoon salt. Sift on top of egg mixture and fold in. Spread evenly over pineapple mixture.

(3) Bake at 375 degrees for 15 to 18 minutes. Cool briefly and loosen edges with point of knife. Sprinkle cake with confectioners' sugar. Place a towel on top of cake and a board on top of towel. Invert. Trim away any crusty edges and roll up from long side. Allow to cool in towel, before placing on serving plate. Serve warm or cold with Gingered Crème Chantilly.

3 eggs
1 cup granulated sugar
¼ cup warm water
1 teaspoon vanilla
1 cup all-purpose flour
1 teaspoon baking powder
¼ teaspoon salt

2 to 4 tablespoons confectioners' sugar

**Gingered Crème Chantilly
(Whipped Cream with Ginger)**

Place 1 cup well chilled whipping cream in chilled small mixer bowl. Beat until beginning to thicken. Add 1 tablespoon confectioners' sugar and 2 tablespoons minced candied ginger* whole continuing to beat. Cease beating when soft peaks form.

*COOK'S TIP: Ginger is a rhizome of a tropical flowering plant. Its spicy flavor can be found in dishes throughout the Oriental menu.

Forms of ginger that can be used in soup and main-dish cooking are the

1 cup whipping cream
1 tablespoon confectioners' sugar
2 tablespoons candied ginger,* minced

whole dried ginger root, ground ginger, bottled juice, or fresh ginger root. Fresh ginger can be used grated, crushed, or sliced. It can be kept indefinitely if frozen, and grated without being thawed.

To flavor desserts, forms of ginger that may be used are either candied or crystallized, and either preserves or marmalade.

Gingered Chicken Broth
Curried Chicken-Lychee Salad
Cold Orange Soufflé

Vouvray Balzac

My very favorite non-green salad is this one featuring cold cubes of chicken in a curry-flavored mayonnaise. The special ingredients called for, such as lychees and honeydew, produce unusual and tantalizing flavor combinations. Equally interesting substitutions are also available to the inventive cook. Instead of lychees you could use canned or fresh green grapes and pineapple rings, or cantaloupe could be substituted for honeydew. At holiday time, leftover turkey makes a most natural substitute for chicken. You may like it so well that in the future you will deliberately create copious amounts of leftover turkey. There is no substitute for chutney; it is the one ingredient which provides continuity of flavor throughout.

The entire "flavor feeling" of this menu reflects taste combinations one would expect to enjoy while island hopping in the China seas. The menu begins with a demitasse of chicken broth which is perfumed with ginger, and ends with a smooth-textured cold orange soufflé. That intrinsic quality of freshness associated with citrus desserts comes through as anticipated. This soufflé is especially handsome as it stands high above the dish and is attractively garnished with sections of mandarin orange.

Although this menu is suggested as a luncheon, it would be perfect to serve on warm summer evenings when dining out-of-doors. The slightly exotic flavors of curry, ginger and tropical fruits suggest hurricane lamps and big, fluffy flowers. Tables skirted right to the patio floor in bright tropical colors, seashells and fish netting, cocktails served from coconut shells — all provide means of altering the environment to accommodate a blissful night of tropical fantasy.

Gingered Chicken Broth

(1) Chill chicken stock from preparation of chicken for salad, and remove solidified fat. Strain stock and bring to simmer. Add 1 slice fresh ginger root and 1 green onion. Simmer 20 minutes. Add 1 tablespoon lemon juice and salt to taste. Strain.

(2) Ladle into demitasse cups for living room service, or have on table when guests sit down.

COOK'S TIP: Substitute undiluted canned chicken broth, if desired. Substitute dry ground ginger to taste, if necessary.

4 cups chicken stock
1 slice ginger root
1 green onion
1 tablespoon lemon juice
Salt to taste

Curried Chicken-Lychee Salad

(1) *Preparation of Chicken* Place 2 whole frying chickens in kettle with water to cover. Add a slice of fresh ginger root, one small whole onion, ½ lemon and 1 teaspoon salt. Simmer covered about 1 hour or until tender. Remove chicken and cool. As soon as it can be handled, separate the meat from the skin and bones. (Return the skin and bones to stock pot

2 (3-pound) frying chickens
1 slice fresh ginger root
1 small onion, peeled
½ lemon
1 teaspoon salt

and simmer until reduced to 4 cups. Reserve for soup.) Cut chicken meat into ½-inch cubes and toss with just enough Sauce Vinaigrette (Page 24) to moisten.

(2) *Dressing* Combine 1 cup mayonnaise, ½ cup dairy sour cream and 2 tablespoons each minced parsley and green onion. Add 1 to 2 teaspoons curry powder. Reserve.

(3) *Additions* Have ready one can (1-pound) drained, whole seedless lychees (green grapes, fresh or canned, may be substituted) and 1½ cups finely diced celery. Refrigerate until serving time.

Final Preparation (1) Add celery and lychees to chicken and stir in sour cream dressing. Taste and add salt if necessary.

(2) Peel two small honeydew melons. Cut in half crosswise and remove seeds. Slice into 8 uniform rings. Place rings on individual plates lined with lettuce leaves. Spoon a mound of the chicken salad on top of each ring. Top with a generous spoonful of chutney.

¼ cup Sauce Vinaigrette (Page 24)

1 cup mayonnaise
½ cup dairy sour cream
2 tablespoons minced parsley
2 tablespoons minced green onion
1 to 2 teaspoons curry powder

1 can (1-pound) whole seedless lychees
1½ cups diced celery

2 small honeydew melons
8 uniform lettuce leaves
1 jar chutney

Cold Orange Souffle

(1) Soften 2 envelopes unflavored gelatin in ½ cup cold water, in top of double boiler. Add two 6-ounce cans concentrated frozen orange juice, ¼ cup sugar and 6 egg yolks. Beat continuously with a stainless wire whisk over simmering water about 8

2 envelopes unflavored gelatin
½ cup cold water
2 cans (6-ounce) concentrated frozen orange juice, undiluted and completely thawed

minutes, or until mixture is smooth and slightly thickened. Remove from heat and stir in 2 tablespoons Grand Marnier. Allow to cool until mixture feels cool to the touch but hasn't begun to set.

¼ cup sugar
6 eggs, separated
2 tablespoons Grand Marnier

COOK'S TIP: You may hasten the cooling by placing pan in ice water and whisking constantly until mixture is cool to the touch.

(2) Add a pinch of salt and ½ teaspoon cream of tartar to 6 egg whites and beat until frothy. Gradually beat in ½ cup sugar. Continue beating until stiff, glossy peaks have formed. Fold cooled yolk mixture into whites.

6 egg whites (from Step 1)
Pinch of salt
½ teaspoon cream of tartar
½ cup sugar

(3) Beat 1 cup whipping cream until thickened but not stiff. Fold into soufflé mixture and spoon into collared one-quart soufflé dish. Chill several hours. Before serving, remove collar and arrange drained mandarin orange sections on top in a spiral design.

1 cup whipping cream
1 can (11-ounce) mandarin orange sections, drained

COOK'S TIP: Cold soufflé mixtures are deliberately proportioned to exceed the capacity of the dish. Cut a strip of waxed paper long enough to wrap around dish and overlap. Fold it in half lengthwise to increase strength. Wrap paper around dish and secure it with paper clips while tying in place with string. Remove clips. Before removing collar run a thin knife between soufflé and waxed paper.

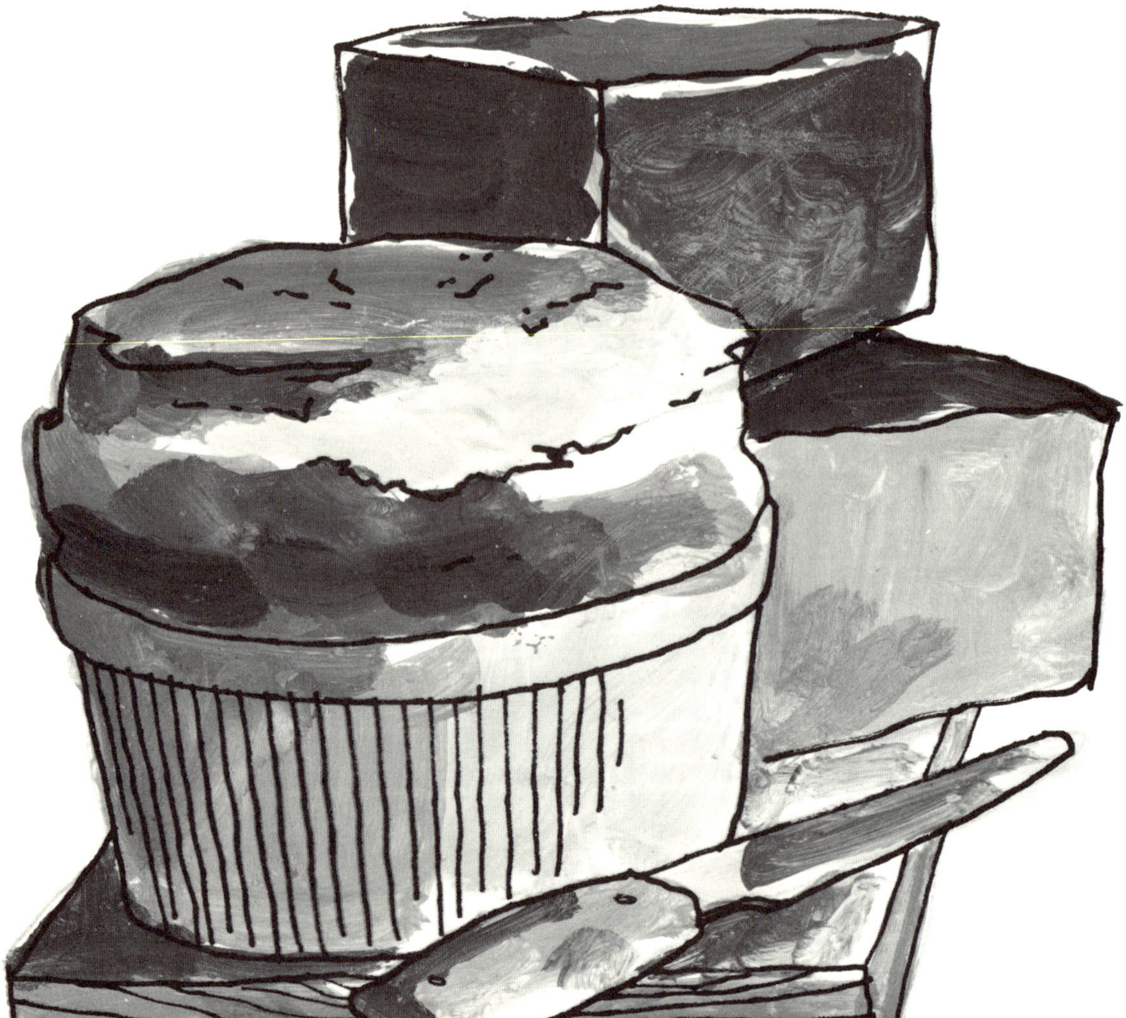

III His and Her Special Menus

All the simple classic dishes thought to be for ladies only. Once the gentlemen have had a taste, they'll insist on being included. Menus for luncheon or late supper.

Asparagus Vinaigrette
Coquilles Saint-Jacques Florentine
Peaches in Raspberry Sauce

White Graves or Muscadet

Maybe you think that people who peel asparagus are just too fussy, but once you've eaten it peeled, chances are you'll never enjoy it otherwise. By peeling asparagus, the cooking time becomes the same for the stalk as it is for the tip. This means it can be cooked completely submerged in boiling water and requires no special equipment.

As a first course, asparagus is often served cold after being marinated in Sauce Vinaigrette. At serving time it is lifted out of its marinade and arranged on lettuce leaves. A classic garnish called Mimosa (included in the menu) is sprinkled on top, with a final garnish of bright red pimento. The dish is irresistible and leaves your guests with high expectations for the courses to follow.

They won't be disappointed. This Florentine version of Coquilles Saint-Jacques is an excellent entrée for a luncheon. Scallops in Sauce Mornay are served on a bed of chopped spinach, with a decorative border of Duchess potatoes. (When Coquilles Saint-Jacques is served as a first course, the potato border may be omitted.)

This beautiful dessert, Peaches in Raspberry Sauce, has been one of the most popular things we've ever done in cooking classes. Quick-thaw frozen peaches are served enveloped in raspberry purée flavored with raspberry brandy. It is topped with fluffy Cognac-flavored whipped cream and garnished with toasted slivers of almond. This dessert is especially pretty when served in a cut glass bowl. It literally sparkles as it is set before your guests.

Asparagus Vinaigrette

Advance Preparation (1) Wash 2 pounds fresh asparagus. Beginning at the blossom end of each stalk, working toward the bottom, remove the scales and skin with a vegetable peeler. Line peeled stalks up and trim away ends evenly, making sure you discard the woody and tough parts of stems.

2 pounds fresh asparagus
Kitchen string
Salted water

(2) To facilitate handling during cooking, divide asparagus into 2 or 3 bundles and tie each bundle in two places with soft kitchen string.

(3) Drop the bundles into boiling salted water (1 teaspoon salt to 1 quart water) and rotate occasionally while simmering, about 8 minutes, or until tender. Remove from water,

1 recipe Sauce Vinaigrette (Page 24)

drain well and remove strings. Lay in flat container and immediately drizzle generously with Sauce Vinaigrette. Refrigerate until serving time.
(4) *Mimosa Garnish* Hard cook one egg and grate into fine particles. Combine with an equal amount of finely minced parsley.
Final Preparation At serving time, drain asparagus and arrange individual servings atop Boston or Bibb lettuce on chilled salad plates. Garnish with Mimosa Garnish and crisscross two strips of pimento at mid-stalk of each serving.

1 hard-cooked egg (Page 25)
Finely minced parsley

Boston or Bibb lettuce
16 strips pimento

Coquilles Saint-Jacques Florentine (Baked Scallops in Mornay Sauce)

Advance Preparation (1) *Spinach* Cook two packages frozen chopped spinach according to package directions. Drain and reserve.
(2) *Scallops* Sauté 1 minced shallot or green onion in 2 tablespoons butter. Add ½ cup dry white wine and bring to simmer. Add 1½ pounds fresh scallops (or frozen scallops completely thawed.) Cook gently about 5 minutes. Remove scallops. Strain and measure poaching liquid. Add enough light cream to make 2 cups. Reserve for Sauce Mornay.
(3) *Potatoes* Prepare 2 cups of instant mashed potatoes according to package directions, adding 2 egg yolks with the liquid.
(4) *Sauce Mornay* Sauté 1 minced

2 packages (10-ounce) frozen chopped spinach

1 shallot, minced
2 tablespoons butter
½ cup dry white wine
1½ pounds scallops
¼ to ½ cup light cream

2 cups prepared instant mashed potatoes
2 egg yolks

1 shallot, minced

shallot in 4 tablespoons butter. Stir in 4 tablespoons flour and cook one minute without browning. Add the scallop liquid from above and whisk until smooth. Season with a grating of nutmeg, ⅛ teaspoon white pepper, and 1 teaspoon salt. Beat together 2 egg yolks and ¼ cup light cream. Whisk into sauce. Add 4 tablespoons grated Parmesan cheese.

Final Preparation Butter 6 to 8 scallop shells. Line the bottoms with a layer of spinach. Add a layer of scallops and mask completely with Sauce Mornay. Sprinkle top lightly with additional grated Parmesan cheese. Spoon the mashed potatoes into a pastry bag and pipe a decorative edge around the outside edge of each scallop shell. Bake at 350 degrees for 30 minutes, or until lightly browned.

- 4 tablespoons butter
- 4 tablespoons flour
- Poaching liquid and cream (Step 2)
- Grating of nutmeg (1/8 teaspoon)
- 1/8 teaspoon white pepper
- 1 teaspoon salt
- 2 egg yolks
- ¼ cup light cream
- 4 tablespoons grated Parmesan cheese

- 6 to 8 scallop shells, 6 inches across
- Additional grated Parmesan cheese, for topping

- Pastry bag

Peaches in Raspberry Sauce

Advance Preparation (1) *Peaches* Open 3 packages quick-thaw frozen sliced peaches. Thaw completely, *drain* and place in glass serving bowl. (2) *Raspberry Sauce* Purée 1 package partially thawed frozen raspberries in blender and force purée through sieve to remove seeds. Stir in 2 tablespoons Framboise or Kirsch. Pour mixture over peaches and refrigerate until serving.

Final Preparation Make one recipe Cognac Chantilly. At serving time, spoon the Cognac Chantilly on top

- 3 packages (10-ounce) quick-thaw frozen sliced peaches

- 1 package (10-ounce) frozen raspberries
- 2 tablespoons Framboise or Kirsch

- 1 recipe Cognac Chantilly (Page 9)

of peaches and garnish with ¼ cup toasted slivered almonds.

¼ cup slivered almonds, toasted

Luncheon Hors-d'Oeuvres
Cannelloni
Petits Pois Pontet Canet
Pots-De-Crème Au Chocolat

California Emerald Riesling

If you can find a set of six or more "raviers" to add to your collection of treasured serving pieces, the wonderful world of French-style hors-d'oeuvres will be open to you. Many of the country inns of France feature a table laden with huge assortments of hors-d'oeuvres foods. Each item is perfectly seasoned and attractively garnished. Served in "raviers," symmetrical and matching oblong dishes, these foods are arranged to complement each other as to color, shape and texture. The visual enjoyment competes favorably with the flavor enjoyment of this presentation.

Advantages of presenting and serving an hors-d'oeuvres course such as this begin to pyramid, considering that many items are made from leftovers. Others improve in flavor when marinated overnight. This means they can be made well ahead. At serving time all you need to do is drain the hors-d'oeuvres and place them in their respective dishes. This course can be served from a side table in the living room. Individual hors-d'oeuvres plates should be provided for guests, who then serve themselves.

Crêpes filled with a variety of meats or seafood combinations make an elegant entrée for a his and her luncheon.* Cannelloni, as presented here, is a French version of an Italian specialty. Minced chicken, delicately seasoned and combined with spinach, provides the filling for crêpes which are baked in a topping of Sauce Mornay. Little French peas, prepared in the style of Chateau Pontet Canet, make a fine vegetable to accompany Cannelloni.

For the wine I have suggested a crisp, fresh white wine.

It is made from the Emerald Riesling, a new grape variety developed by the progressive winegrowers of California.

This luncheon is not one to be eaten in haste. In order to provide the time it deserves, Sunday could be the best day for it, in which case there is little doubt that the gentlemen will insist on joining you. And they will be thrilled with the surprise that awaits them at dessert time. When the cover is removed from their pots-de-crème, they will find a delectable chocolate custard, beguilingly topped with whipped cream and chocolate curls.

*COOK'S TIP: *Seasoning your Crêpe Pan* If you are purchasing a new crêpe pan, it should be washed in sudsy water when you get it home. If it has been coated with a film of oil, it may be necessary to use steel wool to clean it. Next, fill it to the brim with vegetable oil and heat oil on top of stove. Transfer to a 200-degree oven and leave it there overnight. Next day, discard the oil and wipe pan clean with paper towels. *Never* wash again. Wipe with paper towels after use and reserve it for-crêpes-only.

Luncheon Hors-D'Oeuvres (French Style Appetizers)

(1) *Eggs in Mayonnaise* Cut four hard-cooked eggs in half lengthwise and arrange, cut side down in ravier. Thin ¼ cup mayonnaise with 1 tablespoon cream. Add ¼ teaspoon tarragon and spoon mixture over eggs to cover completely. Cut rolled anchovies in half horizontally and decorate each egg with one-half anchovy.

4 hard-cooked eggs (Page 25)
¼ cup mayonnaise
1 tablespoon cream
¼ teaspoon tarragon
4 rolled anchovies

(2) *Marinated Mushroom Caps* Combine ¼ cup white wine vinegar, ¼ cup olive oil, 1 pressed clove garlic, and 1 teaspoon salt. Bring to a simmer and add 1½ cups canned mushroom caps, well drained. Remove

¼ cup white wine vinegar
¼ cup olive oil
1 clove garlic, pressed
1 teaspoon salt
1½ cups mushroom caps (two 4-ounce cans)

from heat and refrigerate overnight in marinade.

(3) *Beets Vinaigrette* Place the contents of one can (1-pound) julienne sliced beets in a saucepan and heat to boiling. Remove from heat, drain, and toss while hot with Sauce Vinaigrette. Refrigerate until serving. Drain and place in ravier.

1 can (1-pound) julienne beets
¼ cup Sauce Vinaigrette (Page 24)

(4) *Carrots Vinaigrette* Peel and slice 4 or 5 carrots into julienne (⅛") strips. Drop into boiling salted water and cook about 3 minutes. Drain and toss while hot with ¼ cup Sauce Vinaigrette. Refrigerate until serving. Drain and place in ravier.

4 or 5 carrots
¼ cup Sauce Vinaigrette (Page 24)

(5) *Celeriac in Caper Sauce* Peel one medium celery root and slice into julienne strips. While working with celeriac, keep it submerged in acidulated water (1 tablespoon vinegar per quart water) to prevent darkening. Drop into boiling salted water. When water returns to boil, remove from heat, drain and toss with Caper Sauce. Refrigerate until serving.

1 medium celery root, peeled and sliced
Acidulated water to cover
Boiling salted water

Caper Sauce Combine ¼ cup mayonnaise, 1 teaspoon Dijon mustard, 1 tablespoon each minced capers and green onion.

¼ cup mayonnaise
1 teaspoon Dijon mustard
1 tablespoon minced capers
1 tablespoon minced green onion

(6) *Cucumbers in Sour Cream* Peel two cucumbers and split lengthwise. Scrape out seeds with spoon. Slice crosswise into thin crescents. Combine 1/3 cup dairy sour cream, ½ teaspoon salt, 1 tablespoon each finely minced green onion and parsley, and a little freshly ground black pep-

2 cucumbers, peeled and sliced
1/3 cup dairy sour cream
½ teaspoon salt
1 tablespoon minced green onion

per. Add the sliced cucumbers and toss. Serve at once, or delay mixing with dressing until ready to serve.

1 tablespoon minced parsley
Freshly ground black pepper

Cannelloni (Chicken Crepes in Mornay Sauce)

Advance Preparation (1) *Crêpes for Entrées* Combine in top of blender: 1 cup cold water, 1 cup milk, 4 eggs, ½ teaspoon salt, 2 cups sifted all-purpose flour, and 4 tablespoons melted butter. Blend well and refrigerate at least 2 hours. Strain batter before frying.

1 cup cold water
1 cup milk
4 eggs
½ teaspoon salt
2 cups all-purpose flour
4 tablespoons melted butter

How to Fry Crêpes Heat a 6-inch crêpe pan or skillet. With a cold chunk of butter wrapped in cheesecloth, quickly rub the bottom of skillet to coat lightly with butter. Spoon in measured amount (2-3 tablespoonful) of crêpe batter to just cover bottom of skillet. Tilt skillet to spread evenly. As soon as *wet look* has disappeared, turn crêpe and continue cooking 1 minute. Turn out on kitchen towel. Stack one on top of the other. Keep lightly covered with towel until ready to fill and roll.

Cheesecloth
Butter

COOK'S TIP: To store crêpes, stack one on top of the other with a piece of waxed paper between each two. Wrap in kitchen towel and place in sealed storage container. Refrigerate or freeze until needed.

(2) *Filling for Crêpes* Combine 2 cups minced cooked chicken, ½

2 cups minced cooked chicken
½ pound sausage meat

pound cooked sausage meat, one package (10-ounce) cooked and drained chopped spinach, and 1 beaten egg. Add ¼ cup grated Parmesan cheese, ½ teaspoon each thyme and salt, and ¼ teaspoon white pepper. Stir in ½ cup Sauce Mornay (below) and reserve.

1 package (10-ounce) frozen chopped spinach, cooked and drained
¼ cup grated Parmesan cheese
1 beaten egg
½ teaspoon thyme
½ teaspoon salt
¼ teaspoon white pepper

(3) *Sauce Mornay* Heat 4 tablespoons butter and sauté 1 minced shallot or green onion. Add 4 tablespoons flour and cook one minute without browning. Whisk in 2 cups milk. Add 1 teaspoon salt, ⅛ teaspoon white pepper, and a grating of nutmeg. Continue cooking until thickened and smooth. Beat together 2 egg yolks and ¼ cup light cream. Whisk into sauce. Stir in 2 to 4 tablespoons grated Parmesan cheese. Add ½ cup sauce to filling mixture from Step 2.

4 teaspoons butter
1 minced shallot or green onion
4 tablespoons flour
2 cups milk
1 teaspoon salt
1/8 teaspoon white pepper
Grating of nutmeg (1/8 teaspoon)
2 egg yolks
¼ cup light cream
2 to 4 tablespoons grated Parmesan cheese

Final Preparation Place 2 tablespoons chicken mixture on each crêpe and roll. Place rolls snugly against one another in buttered baking dish. Spread with remaining Sauce Mornay.* Sprinkle top lightly with additional grated cheese. Bake at 350 degrees for 20 to 25 minutes.

1 tablespoon grated Parmesan cheese for top

*COOK'S TIP: Sauce Mornay has a tendency to thicken upon standing, as the gluten in the flour expands. If this happens, thin it down with milk.

Petits Pois Pontet Canet (Tiny Green Peas with Ham and Shallots)

(1) In a large skillet sauté 2 to 4 tablespoons finely minced ham and one minced shallot in 2 tablespoons butter. Remove from heat and add ¼ teaspoon thyme, a sprig of parsley and 2 packages frozen tiny peas, partially thawed. Sprinkle with 1 teaspoon salt. Reserve.

(2) Just before serving time cover peas with whole lettuce leaves. Simmer gently for about 5 minutes. Lift lettuce leaves and stir once. When peas are tender, discard lettuce and parsley. Stir in an additional tablespoon of butter and continue cooking until peas are glazed.

2 to 4 tablespoons minced ham
1 shallot, minced
2 tablespoons butter
¼ teaspoon thyme
1 sprig parsley
2 packages (10-ounce) frozen tiny peas
1 teaspoon salt

1 or 2 lettuce leaves
1 tablespoon butter

Pots-de-Crème au Chocolat (Chocolate Custard in Little Pots)

Advance Preparation (1) In saucepan heat 3 cups light cream, ¾ cup sugar and 2 squares chopped unsweetened chocolate. Stir constantly until chocolate has melted.

(2) Meanwhile, beat 6 egg yolks with 1 teaspoon vanilla until well blended. Continuing to beat with a wire whisk, gradually add the hot cream mixture. Strain and pour into eight 4-ounce pots-de-crème, or custard cups.

(3) Place pots-de-crème in a pan and fill pan with hot water to a depth of 1½-2 inches. Bake at 325 degrees for 30 minutes. Remove from oven, cool, and refrigerate several hours.

3 cups light cream
¾ cup sugar
2 squares unsweetened chocolate, chopped

6 egg yolks
1 teaspoon vanilla

Final Preparation Beat ½ cup whipping cream with 1 tablespoon sugar until fairly stiff. Spoon into a pastry bag and decorate each serving with a rosette of whipped cream. Garnish each rosette with a crystalized violet or curls of chocolate. Place lids on pots and let the guests discover for themselves the beautiful surprise inside.

COOK'S TIP I: To make chocolate curls, let a 1-ounce square of semisweet chocolate stand in warm place to soften slightly. With a vegetable peeler make thin slices from broad surface of chocolate. Chill before handling.

COOK'S TIP II: Sets of pots-de-crème or custard pots with covers may be purchased at department or specialty stores. Or, any attractive 4-ounce ovenproof dishes may be used.

½ cup whipping cream
1 tablespoon sugar
8 crystallized violets, or several chocolate curls

Cucumber Vichyssoise
Ham and Asparagus Roulades with Béarnaise
Coeur à la Crème with Strawberries

Tavel Rosé

By now it has no doubt become apparent that you must either buy a blender or live next door to a kind neighbor who has one. So many recipes make use of it that it has become essential to today's cookery methods. It is called into service in this menu to make an up-to-date version of Vichyssoise. Frozen potato soup is puréed in the blender. Puréed fresh cucumbers are added to produce a summery quality. This soup is best when served icy cold. If you have icers, now is the time to use them.

The familiar flavors of ham and asparagus are pleasantly accented with Sauce Béarnaise and its tangy wine and tarragon. This sauce is also made in the blender. Ham and Asparagus Roulades make a fetching entrée for this luncheon, but they can also be served as a sophisticated first course at other times.

In France, during summer months, tiny fresh strawberries are sometimes served with soft fresh cheeses which are molded into the shape of a heart. This elegant dessert, known as Coeur à la Crème, can be duplicated here with a combination of cottage cheese, cream cheese and whipping cream. It's best to make it the day before, which is a "do ahead" feature in its favor.

This menu is suggested for a summer luncheon. Wouldn't it be fun to decorate with bouquets of fresh garden vegetables? For contrast, try tying them into bundles with pastel satin ribbons, letting the ribbons trail across the table. A pretty white cloth is called for as well as your best crystal and china.

Cucumber Vichyssoise (Cold Potato Soup with Cucumber)

(1) Place 2 cans partially thawed frozen potato soup in top of blender. Add 2 cans chicken broth and one soup can of milk. Blend well. Transfer to saucepan, heat to boiling and remove from heat.

2 cans (10-ounce) frozen, or canned, potato soup
2 cans (10½-ounce) chicken broth
1 soup can milk

(2) Peel and seed 2 medium cucumbers. Purée in blender and stir into hot soup mixture. Add a dash of Tabasco. Chill well.

2 medium cucumbers
Dash of Tabasco

(3) Just before serving, stir in ½ cup heavy cream. Serve in icers garnished with minced chives.

½ cup heavy cream
Minced chives

Ham and Asparagus Roulades
(Ham and Asparagus Rolls)

Advance Preparation (1) Prepare 2 pounds of asparagus by cooking directions on page 44. When asparagus is tender remove from boiling water, wrap in kitchen towel and reserve.

2 pounds fresh asparagus (How to cook, page 44)

(2) Trim crusts from white bread, 1 slice per serving. Take off 1-inch triangle from 2 opposite corners, creating an elongated hexagon. (Accommodates length of the asparagus.) Brush both sides with melted butter and toast at 350 degrees for 12 to 15 minutes, turning once.

8 slices white bread
¼ pound melted butter

(3) Prepare 1 recipe Sauce Béarnaise (follows) and have ready one thin slice of boiled ham per serving.

1 recipe Sauce Béarnaise
8 thin slices boiled ham

Final Preparation Roll several spears of asparagus into each slice of ham. Place each roll on prepared toast. Pour a ribbon of Béarnaise at midstalk of each serving. Place on baking sheet and bake at 350 degrees for 5 to 8 minutes, or hold in a warm oven (lowest setting) up to 30 minutes.

Sauce Béarnaise (Hot Butter-Egg Sauce with Tarragon)

(1) *Prepare Concentrate* Combine in saucepan ¼ cup white wine vinegar, ¼ cup dry white wine, 1 tablespoon minced shallot, 1 teaspoon tarragon, ½ teaspoon salt and a dash of Tabasco. Cook until mixture is reduced to 2 tablespoons concentrate.

¼ cup white wine vinegar
¼ cup dry white wine
1 tablespoon minced shallot
1 teaspoon tarragon
½ teaspoon salt
Dash of Tabasco

(2) Place the 2 tablespoons concen-

Concentrate (from Step 1)

trate in warmed blender container. Add 4 egg yolks. Blend briefly. Continuing to blend, pour 1 cup hot clarified butter in a slow steady stream into natural whirlpool formed by spinning blades of blender. Cease blending when mixture has thickened and all butter is incorporated. Taste and add a little extra tarragon and Tabasco if necessary to sharpen flavor. Cover and place blender container in warm water until needed.

4 egg yolks
1 cup clarified butter (Page 15)

Coeur à la Crème with Strawberries (Cream Cheese Heart with Strawberries)

Advance Preparation (1) *Cheese* Beat together two 8-ounce packages softened cream cheese, 2 cups small-curd cream-style cottage cheese and 1 cup whipping cream. Continue beating until very smooth.

2 packages (8-ounce) cream cheese
2 cups small-curd cream-style cottage cheese
1 cup whipping cream

(2) Line a 6 or 8-inch heart-shaped mold with wet cheesecloth.* Spoon in cheese mixture and overlap the outer edges of the cheesecloth to completely cover top of cheese. Place mold on a plate to drain and refrigerate overnight.

1 square (18-inch) cheesecloth
1 heart-shaped mold (6 or 8-inch)*

*COOK'S TIP: Individual sized heart-shaped molds, made either of porcelain or straw, are available in most gourmet shops. Larger 6 to 8-inch straw baskets are useful to serve several guests. To make your own mold, buy an 8-inch aluminum heart-shaped layer cake pan. Perforate the bottom generously with an ice pick or with a hammer and nail.

Final Preparation Service Method I
(1) Wash, but do not remove hulls from 2 pints fresh, whole strawberries. Place in a bowl and drizzle with 2 tablespoons Kirsch. Sprinkle with about ½ cup sugar, tasting to determine the desired degree of sweetness.

2 pints strawberries
2 tablespoons Kirsch
½ cup sugar

(2) Unmold the Coeur á la Crème on a serving dish and surround it with a ring of whole, sugared strawberries. The top may be garnished with sliced strawberries. Cut sections of the heart with a pie server and transfer to dessert plates. Add several whole strawberries to each serving.

Service Method II Strawberry Sauce*
Wash and hull 2 pints fresh, whole strawberries. Place all but 1 cup of the berries in a bowl and drizzle with 2 tablespoons Kirsch. Sprinkle with sugar to taste. Place the reserved 1 cup of berries in the container of blender and purée them while adding ½ cup melted red currant jelly. Pour the purée over the whole berries. Place in a side dish to be spooned over servings of Coeur à la Crème.

2 pints strawberries
2 tablespoons Kirsch
Sugar to taste
½ cup red currant jelly

*Cook's Tip: This is an excellent fresh Strawberry Sauce to use as a topping for ice cream, plain cakes, or even as a filling for crêpes.

Sherried Beef Broth on the Rocks
Cheese Soufflé   Mixed Grilled Vegetables
Blueberries in Sour Cream

California Sylvaner or Traminer

First courses that can be served to guests in the living room have many advantages. One of these is the ease with which they can be served. Consommés, hot or cold, are great for this purpose.

Sherried beef broth on the rocks is my choice to precede the cheese soufflé in this menu. When you serve the beef broth, you can announce that the soufflé will soon be ready. This way, everyone is kept occupied while waiting and yet they are made aware of your timing needs. Soufflés should be served as soon as possible after being removed from the oven. Everything else should be ready and waiting.

Rather than belabor the fine points of soufflé making, let me assure you that experience is by far the best teacher. If you start with a dependable recipe, as the one included here, you should enjoy success with your very first soufflé. Just remember that the instructions should be followed *exactly as outlined*. Ingredients should be added *when specified,* and recipes geared to the capacity of the dish. (This one is for a 2-quart dish.) There is no reason to be fearful of making a soufflé and you will find it a rewarding experience.

Mixed grilled vegetables will be a fine addition to your repertoire of standard recipes. They are superb with this entrée, and they are equally enjoyable with grilled steaks or chops.

When summer fruits are combined with sour cream and brown sugar you are doubly rewarded. As the sugar dissolves, it combines with the cream to produce a lovely caramel sauce which is excellent with blueberries, strawberries or seedless grapes. Take advantage of each fruit as it comes into season for a dessert that will be an instant success.

Sherried Beef Broth on the Rocks

Fill 8 old fashioned glasses with ice cubes. Add ½ ounce dry sherry to each. Fill with full strength canned beef bouillon. Garnish each serving with a twist of lemon.

Ice cubes
Dry cocktail sherry
4 cans (10½-ounce) beef bouillon
8 lemon twists

Cheese Soufflé

(1) *Soufflé Base* Heat 4 tablespoons butter in saucepan and sauté 1 minced shallot. Add 4 tablespoons flour and cook one minute without browning. Whisk in 2 cups milk. Add 1 teaspoon salt, ⅛ teaspoon white pepper, and a grating of nutmeg. Continue cooking until thickened and smooth.

(2) Beat 6 egg yolks well and whisk into Soufflé Base. Whisk 1½ cups mixed shredded cheeses into mixture. Cool to room temperature.

Cook's Tip: Preparation to this point can be done early in the day. Cover Soufflé Base and keep at room temperature. Place egg whites in large mixer bowl. Cover with plate and leave at room temperature. Forty-five minutes before serving, proceed with Step 3.

(3) Add a dash salt and ½ teaspoon cream of tartar to 7 egg whites in large mixer bowl. Beat until frothy. Continue beating until whites hold firms peaks but do not appear dry. Stir one-third of beaten whites into soufflé mixture until well blended. Add remaining whites carefully, folding in with rubber spatula.

4 tablespoons butter
1 shallot, minced
4 tablespoons flour
2 cups milk
1 teaspoon salt
1/8 teaspoon white pepper
Grating of nutmeg (1/8 teaspoon)

6 egg yolks
1½ cups mixed shredded cheese (Swiss, Romano, Parmesan, Fontina, or Gruyère

7 egg whites
Dash salt
½ teaspoon cream of *tartar*

(4) Butter bottom and sides of a 2-quart soufflé dish and dust with 1 tablespoon grated Parmesan cheese. Spoon soufflé mixture into dish. Sprinkle top with additional 1 tablespoon grated cheese. Place in bottom third of a 400-degree oven. Remove top shelf. Immediately reduce temperature to 375 degrees. Bake 35 or 40 minutes until set. Serve as soon as possible.

2-quart soufflé dish
2 tablespoons grated Parmesan cheese

Mixed Grilled Vegetables

Advance Preparation Peel one large Spanish onion and slice into vertical slivers from the root end, discarding root itself. Remove seeds from 2 green peppers and slice into julienne strips. Wash and trim 1 pound fresh mushrooms. Slice thinly from stem end through cap. Remove hard core from 3 or 4 tomatoes and slice into wedges.

1 large Spanish onion
2 green bell peppers
1 pound fresh mushrooms
3 or 4 tomatoes

Final Preparation Twenty minutes prior to serving, heat 2 tablespoons butter and 2 tablespoons oil in skillet. Add onions, sprinkle with salt to taste, and cook, covered, 8 to 10 minutes. (As each layer of vegetables is added sprinkle lightly with salt.) Remove cover and add green peppers.* When heated through, add mushrooms. Cook about 4 minutes. Add tomatoes and cease cooking as soon as tomatoes are heated through.

2 tablespoons butter
2 tablespoons oil
Salt to taste

*COOK'S TIP: Do not re-cover dish after addition of green peppers so that peppers remain green. If you must hold dish, leave cover ajar so that steam is not trapped in pan.

Blueberries in Sour Cream

Wash and hull 2 pounds fresh blueberries.* Sort and discard bruised or unsound berries. Drain well and combine with 1 cup dairy sour cream. Spoon into stemmed dessert dishes. Sprinkle generously with brown sugar.

*COOK'S TIP: When blueberries are not in season, substitute 2 pounds Thompson seedless grapes, or 2 pints **sliced** strawberries flavored with 1 **tablespoon** dark rum.

2 pounds blueberries*
1 cup dairy sour cream
½ cup brown sugar

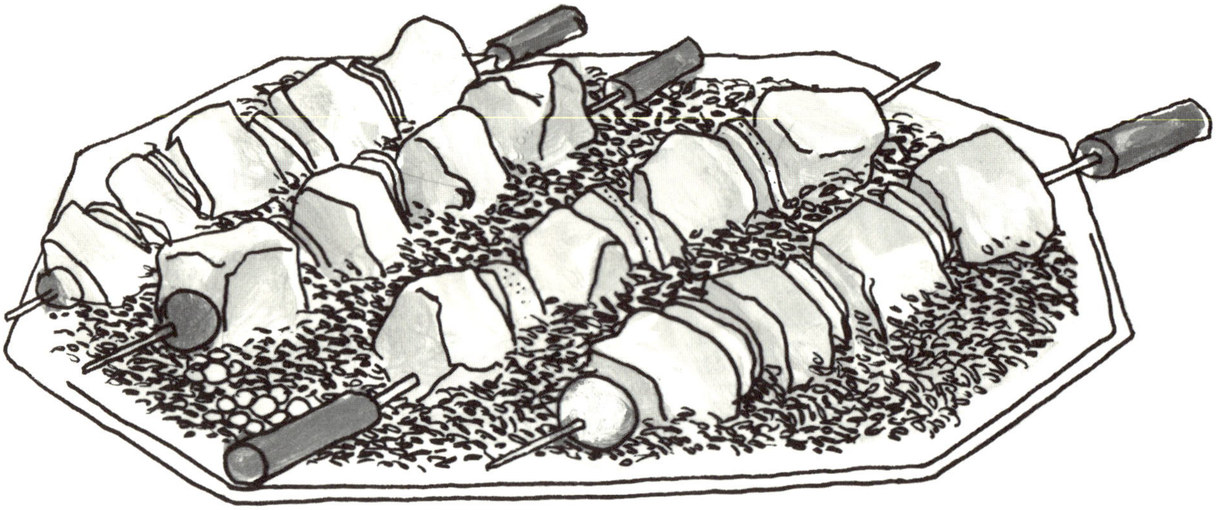

IV ALL ABOARD: PASSPORTS, PLEASE

All aboard for an adventurous tour of foreign specialties. An interpretation of cuisines which are typical of Spain, the Middle East, Russia and India.

Gazpacho
Paella a la Valenciana
Flan con Salsa Caramelo

—

White Spanish Rioja
or
Red California Mountain Burgundy

To travel in Spain is to fall in love with gazpacho. As when falling in love, making the right choice is everything. Actually, you might find choosing the right mate easier than choosing the right gazpacho. There are countless versions of this classic tomato soup, which is served icy cold.

Normally, the ingredients used to make gazpacho — tomatoes, green peppers, onions, garlic, et cetera — are not cooked. In the version included here, the onion and garlic *are* cooked before being combined with the remaining ingredients. By using canned tomatoes one can consistently produce a soup which has a true red color. This version is served surrounded with a variety of condiments, most of which were included in the basic soup. Thus, guests may create their own favorite gazpacho by adding an assortment of condiments as desired. This version of gazpacho appeals to a wide range of taste preferences and the method of service adds much to the festive feeling of the party.

Paella, the classic "Spanish rice", which is found in the area of Valencia, contains chicken and shellfish as well as ham, sausage and vegetables. This abundant variety of ingredients makes paella a popular one-dish party entrée. With advance organization as outlined here, you can finish this beautiful presentation and have it ready to serve in about thirty minutes.

You may expand this menu by the addition of toasted garlic bread and a tossed green salad. Either a light red or dry white wine is suitable to serve with this paella.

For dessert, you will enjoy egg custard baked in caramel sauce, which is known as flan in Spain. This dessert is simplicity itself to make and it produces a "just right" texture-flavor combination to follow paella.

Although you will find this menu enjoyable year round, it is an excellent one to serve at a late day summer gathering. As your guests are arriving, perhaps you might like to serve Sangria (recipe in Amigos de Mexico). Should the host be moved to propose a toast, let it be the Spanish one, "Salud, suerte y amor, y el tiempo para gozarlos" — health, luck and love, and the time to enjoy it!

Gazpacho (Cold Tomato Soup with Condiments)

Advance Preparation (1) *Soup* Heat 2 tablespoons olive oil in covered saucepan. Chop and add 2 large Spanish onions and 2 pressed cloves garlic. Cook 5 minutes, covered. Cool and

2 tablespoons olive oil
2 large Spanish onions, chopped
2 cloves garlic, pressed

place in top of blender. Add one large can Italian tomatoes, 1 teaspoon salt, 1 teaspoon paprika and 2 tablespoons red wine vinegar. Blend until smooth. Stir in 1 can condensed chicken broth. Refrigerate until icy cold.

(2) *Condiments* Prepare ¾ cup finely minced parsley, ¾ cup finely minced green onion, 1 can chopped ripe olives, 2 diced tomatoes, 1 peeled and seeded diced cucumber, 1 diced green pepper, and 1 cup tiny crisp garlic croutons. Place ingredients in individual bowls.

Final Preparation and Service Place chilled soup in large bowl with ladle. Arrange bowls of prepared condiments around base of Gazpacho. As servings are ladled into individual bowls, allow guests to select choice of condiments.

1 can (1-pound 14-ounce) Italian tomatoes
1 teaspoon salt
1 teaspoon paprika
2 tablespoons red wine vinegar
1 can (10½-ounce) chicken broth
¾ cup finely minced parsley
¾ cup finely minced green onion
1 can (4-ounce) chopped ripe olives
2 tomatoes, diced
1 cucumber, peeled, seeded and diced
1 green bell pepper, diced
1 cup tiny crisp garlic croutons

Paella à la Valenciana (Spanish Rice in the Style of Valencia)

Advance Preparation (1) *Chicken* Disjoint one 3-pound frying chicken and cut into 8 servings. Combine 1 teaspoon oregano, ½ teaspoon freshly ground black pepper, 1 pressed clove garlic, 1 teaspoon salt, 1 tablespoon red wine vinegar and 2 tablespoons olive oil. Add chicken and toss to coat evenly. Marinate overnight or a minimum of 3 to 4 hours.

(2) *Pre-Cooking Chicken* Heat 2 tablespoons olive oil in cast iron skillet. Brown pieces of chicken evenly on all

1 (3-pound) frying chicken
1 teaspoon oregano
½ teaspoon freshly ground black pepper
1 clove garlic, pressed
1 teaspoon salt
1 tablespoon red wine vinegar
2 tablespoons olive oil

2 tablespoons olive oil

sides. Leave chicken in skillet and place in a 375-degree oven. Bake, uncovered, for 45 minutes, turning once. Reserve.

(3) *Seafood* Sauté 2 minced green onions in 1 tablespoon olive oil. Add ½ cup dry white wine. Add 1 pound shelled and deveined shrimp. Split 4 lobster tails in half and lay on top of shrimp. Simmer 6 to 8 minutes. Remove seafood and reserve liquid. Have on hand, but do not cook, 8 or more fresh clams in the shell.

2 green onions, minced
1 tablespoon olive oil
½ cup dry white wine
1 pound shelled and deveined shrimp
4 lobster tails, split
8 or more fresh clams in the shell

(4) *Chicken Bouillon* Make 4 cups chicken bouillon from cubes. Combine with liquid from seafood. Add ¼ teaspoon powdered saffron, and ½ teaspoon ground coriander. Reserve.

4 cups chicken bouillon
¼ teaspoon powdered saffron
½ teaspoon ground coriander

(5) *Ham and Sausage* Slice ½ pound ham into strips. Sauté in 1 teaspoon olive oil. Add ¼ pound chorizo or pepperoni. Cook through and reserve.

½ pound ham, slivered
1 teaspoon olive oil
¼ pound chorizo or pepperoni

(6) *Additions* Assemble on a tray and place near cooking area ¼ cup olive oil, 1 large chopped Spanish onion, 2 cloves garlic and garlic press, 1 bottle drained capers, 1 can drained, chopped pimento, ½ package tiny frozen peas and 2 cups converted rice.

¼ cup olive oil
1 large Spanish onion, chopped
2 cloves garlic
1 bottle capers, drained
1 can (4-ounce) pimento, chopped and drained
½ package (13-ounce) tiny frozen peas
2 cups converted rice

Final Preparation and Service Thirty minutes before serving time, heat an 18-inch paella pan. Utilizing all prepared ingredients, begin by adding ¼ cup olive oil. Add chopped onion and pressed garlic. Sauté briefly and stir in rice. When rice is well coated with oil, add ham and sausage. Heat through. Add chicken pieces and heat through. Add the shrimp and toss all together. Add capers and pimento. Heat chicken stock mixture to boiling. Pour over contents of paella pan. Arrange lobster tails in a spiral design on top of rice. Intersperse clams at random. Cover pan with a tent of aluminum foil. Place in a 400-degree oven for 25 minutes. Remove cover and scatter peas over top. Continue baking (5 to 6 minutes) until liquid is absorbed. Serve from paella pan.

Flan con Salsa Caramelo
(Custard with Caramel Sauce)

Advance Preparation (1) *Caramel* Place 1 cup granulated sugar in a cast iron skillet. Stir with a wooden spoon over moderate heat until sugar has melted and turned golden. Pour caramel into a 4 or 6-cup charlotte mold (or bread loaf pan). Turn to coat inside of mold evenly.

(2) *Flan* Beat together 6 eggs, ½ cup sugar, 1 teaspoon vanilla and 2½ cups evaporated milk (or scalded light cream). Strain mixture and pour into prepared mold. Place mold in a baking dish or roaster half-filled with hot water. Bake at 350 degrees for 1 hour or until knife blade can be inserted and withdrawn clean. Cool and refrigerate until serving time.

Final Preparation Run tip of knife around top of flan. Invert on serving dish. Add 2 tablespoons water to

1 cup granulated sugar

6 eggs
½ cup sugar
1 teaspoon vanilla
2½ cups evaporated milk (or scalded light cream)

2 tablespoons water

mold, and heat gently over hot water until remaining caramel has dissolved. Pour over flan. Cut into wedges. Spoon a little caramel sauce over each serving.

Tabouleh
Lamb Shish Kebab
Middle Eastern Pilaf
Oven-Grilled Eggplant and Tomato
Melon and Orange Sherbet

California Cabernet Sauvignon

If you've never had tabouleh, you are in for an exciting culinary experience. Cracked wheat is combined with extravagant amounts of minced parsley, green onion, and tomato. After being combined, these ingredients are seasoned with olive oil and lemon juice. Then the tabouleh is refrigerated overnight so that the flavors mellow and adjust to one another. The flavor is memorable and so is the texture. Tabouleh is a great prelude to a summer cook-out, especially one featuring lamb.

Lamb shish kebab is a natural to follow tabouleh. Marinated cubes of lamb and vegetables can be placed on skewers well in advance of your party. Cooking is a minimal chore, as the kebabs can be broiled in the oven or cooked over a charcoal fire out of doors. Guests may even take over their own cooking when dining outside. Either way, the shish kebabs are served with an unusual pilaf of Middle Eastern origin. This rice dish contains a pasta product known as Rosa Marina, and the cooking method is a little out of the ordinary. Even if you cannot locate Rosa Marina, you are urged to proceed without it, for the final embellishment of browned butter gives this rice a unique flavor.

The demands for authentic flavor in a recipe and minimum effort in the method are never ending. It is a happy cook who can meet such demands creatively as we do with this recipe for oven-grilled eggplant. Eggplant is simply sliced, encased in an ingenious seasoned crust, and baked. Each serving is self-contained and looks very pretty on the plate with other foods.

Tabouleh and shish kebab share a common cultural heritage with melon, which can be served in many interesting ways. For this menu cantaloupe is drizzled with orange liqueur and topped with orange sherbet. This offers a cool and refreshing flavor for ending summer dinners.

This menu is easy to expand and I use it for a seated buffet for sixteen. Decorating for this party menu is fun! I sort through my Christmas decorations for hand carved camels and turbaned Wise Men. They are used with candles to create a centerpiece which resembles an oasis in the desert. Shocking pink tablecloths, accented with burnt orange napkins, and all-white china complete the setting. This creates an elegant atmosphere in which to enjoy these Middle Eastern specialties.

Tabouleh (Middle-Eastern Cracked Wheat Salad)

(1) *Bulgur Wheat* Wash 1 cup cracked bulgur wheat through several changes of water. Pour boiling water to cover over cracked wheat and let stand ½ hour. Drain and squeeze dry.

(2) *Additions* Prepare and add to cracked wheat 1 pound diced fresh tomatoes, 1 cup minced green onion and 3 to 4 cups minced parsley. Toss all ingredients together.

(3) *Dressing* Combine 1/3 cup fresh lemon juice, 1 teaspoon salt and a little freshly ground black pepper. Add ½ cup olive oil and beat to blend. Stir into wheat mixture. Place in tightly covered container and re-

1 cup cracked bulgur wheat
Boiling water to cover

1 pound fresh tomatoes, diced
1 cup minced green onion
3 to 4 cups minced parsley

1/3 cup fresh lemon juice
1 teaspoon salt
Freshly ground black pepper
½ cup olive oil
8 lettuce cups, optional

frigerate overnight or at least several hours. Serve as first course in small bowls or lettuce cups.

Lamb Shish Kebab

Advance Preparation (1) *Marinade* Combine ¼ cup each lemon juice and dry red wine. Add 1 pressed clove garlic, 1 teaspoon salt, ½ teaspoon oregano, 1 teaspoon crushed bay leaf and ½ teaspoon marjoram. Blend in ½ cup olive oil.

(2) *Lamb* Allowing 2 to 3 cubes of lamb per skewer, cut a 5 to 6-pound leg of lamb into 1½ to 2-inch cubes. Place in marinade and refrigerate overnight, turning occasionally.

(3) *Vegetables* Seed and quarter 4 green bell peppers. Cut each quarter in half. Peel 24 small whole onions and drop into boiling salted water to cover for 5 minutes. (Or select 24 small whole onions of uniform size from packaged frozen onions.) Cut 2 lemons into quarters.

Final Preparation Broiling Shish Kebabs Alternate cubes of lamb on 12 inch skewers with pieces of green pepper and onion. Reserve marinade. Place a wedge of lemon on skewer last and push snug against the last item on the skewer. Sprinkle skewered items with freshly ground black pepper. Place skewers on rack 6 inches below broiler.* Broil for 15 minutes, turning several times and basting with
*May be cooked on outdoor grill.

¼ *cup fresh lemon juice*
¼ *cup dry red wine*
1 clove garlic, pressed
1 teaspoon salt
½ *teaspoon oregano*
1 teaspoon crushed bay leaf
½ *teaspoon marjoram*
½ *cup olive oil*

5 to 6-pound leg of lamb

4 green bell peppers
24 small whole onions
2 lemons, quartered

Freshly ground black pepper

the marinade. Arrange Kebabs on bed of Middle Eastern Pilaf.

Middle Eastern Pilaf

(1) Place 2 tablespoons butter in heavy kettle and heat until foamy. Add ½ cup Rosa Marina No. 35.* and cook until butter and pasta are lightly browned. Wash 2 cups long grain rice through several changes of water, drain and shake dry. Add to Rosa Marina and cook 2 to 3 minutes, stirring constantly.

(2) Combine 4 teaspoons instant chicken bouillon with 4 cups hot water. Pour into rice mixture. Cover tightly and bring to rapid boil. Reduce heat to lowest setting and cook 15 minutes. Remove from heat and leave covered until ready to serve. Transfer to heated serving platter.

(3) Place 4 tablespoons butter in saucepan and place over heat. Stir constantly until butter turns a deep golden brown. Pour evenly over Pilaf.

*COOK'S TIP: Rosa Marina No. 35, also known as Orzo, is a pasta, shaped to resemble an oversized grain of rice. It is available in Italian and Greek grocery stores. If you are unable to locate it, proceed with recipe using rice only. Reduce water to 3 cups.

2 tablespoons butter
½ cup Rosa Marina No. 35*
2 cups washed long grain rice

4 teaspoons instant chicken bouillon
4 cups water

4 tablespoons butter, browned

Oven-Grilled Eggplant and Tomato

Advance Preparation (1) *Crumbs* Run enough herb-seasoned salad crou-

1 cup fine, herb-seasoned bread crumbs

tons through blender to make 1 cup fine crumbs. Reserve.

(2) Select one slender, medium-sized eggplant and cut into ½-inch rounds without removing peel. Sprinkle with salt on both sides and let stand one-half hour. Make 8 uniform, ¼-inch slices of tomato (3-inch or one as large in circumference as the eggplant).

(3) Blot egg plant dry with paper towels. Spread each side with a thin coating of garlic mayonnaise. Press into crumbs to coat evenly. Lay on oiled baking sheet. Place a slice of tomato on each, and spread tomato lightly with garlic mayonnaise. Sprinkle with additional crumbs, pressing them in somewhat. Set aside until 20 minutes before serving time.

Final Preparation Place in a 425-degree oven and bake, without turning, 20 minutes.

8 slices (½-inch) unpeeled eggplant

8 slices (¼-inch) large tomatoes

½ cup mayonnaise, combined with 1 pressed clove garlic

Melon and Orange Sherbet

(1) Just prior to serving, cut 2 cantaloupes into quarters and remove seeds. Drizzle each quarter with Grand Marnier or other orange-flavored liqueur. Leave at room temperature.

(2) At serving time place a ball of orange sherbet on each quartered cantaloupe.

(3) Cut 8 large strawberries in half from stem through tip and place one half on either side of sherbet, with points toward points of cantaloupe.

2 cantaloupes, quartered
4 to 6 tablespoons Grand Marnier

1 quart orange sherbet

8 strawberries, split lengthwise
16 tiny sprigs mint

Arrange small sprigs of mint at base of each sliced strawberry to resemble natural leaf top.

Herring in Sour Cream   *Pickled Beets*
Salade Olivier   *Deviled Eggs and Caviar*
White Bean Salad   *Cucumbers in Sour Cream*
Black Bread and Butter
Mrs. Conlin's Best Borsch
Pirozhky
Sultana Cake

When you find yourself in the depths of winter, and snow is accumulating at an alarming rate, you may as well relax and enjoy it. Don your best babushka, tie sleigh bells to the door and invite everyone in for a Doctor Zhivago kind of evening.

Although you might hesitate to build a menu around soup, you will find this version of borsch to be adequate for even the heartiest of appetites. It is preceded by a generous array of Russian hors-d'oeuvres which are called, collectively, zakusky. In selecting foods for zakusky, one learns that the Russian cuisine, like ours in America, reflects tastes of settlers from many different cultural backgrounds. Even some French influence is found in the cuisine, which dates from the days when the Czars of Russia employed fine French chefs.

This zakusky course borrows flavors from Russia's Scandinavian neighbors on the west: sour cream, dill, cucumbers, and herring. The French touch is apparent in Salade Olivier. You will also garnish deviled eggs with Russia's beloved caviar and make an unusual white bean salad. All of these foods go well with black bread and butter. This course can be enjoyed in the living room during a "home-style" cocktail hour. Include a vodka drink or two for good measure.

As for the borsch,* this is a "composite" recipe which has evolved from the various ethnic concepts of the dish. It reflects the characteristic flavors of borsch, which are delicately *sweet* and *sour*. It is the good red color of beets and also contains cabbage. It contains lots of beef, and each serving is topped with sour cream and it is eaten with little meat turnovers, known as pirozhky.

One can't help wondering why other great soups of the world don't have a counterpart of pirozhky. In this shortcut version, turnover crust is made from refrigerated crescent dinner rolls. The filling is made from beef which is pleasantly flavored with dill. Pirozhky, hot from the oven, are eaten along with borsch instead of bread or crackers.

Dried fruits are often found in Russian desserts. This lovely raisin cake, although not typically Russian, is entirely appropriate as a dessert for this menu. It can be enjoyed with tea, or you might enjoy serving it with a compote of warm winter fruits. Just do as the Russian homemaker might do; go to your cupboard and combine whatever canned or dried fruits you have on hand — peaches, pears, apricots and/or cooked dried prunes. Warm them in a chafing dish and lace the syrup generously with fruit brandies.

Who cares if the snow is flying? You can create a cozy atmosphere to remember all summer long.

*Cook's Tip: It is a good idea to begin cooking main dish soups which contain meat or poultry the day before needed. Refrigerate meat and soup stock overnight. When cold, cooked meat is easier to trim. Fat will have solidified and can be removed easily from soup stock.

Zakusky

Russian appetizers may be served in raviers (see page 47) or in interesting serving dishes of assorted sizes. Set up buffet service in the living room, providing hors-d'oeuvres plates and forks for guests. Serve with black bread and butter.

Herring in Sour Cream and Pickled Beets

These items may be purchased ready-made.

2 jars (8-ounce) Herring in Sour Cream
1 jar (16-ounce) pickled beets

Salade Olivier

Advance Preparation (1) Pare, trim and cut the following ingredients into ¼-inch dice: 3 medium boiled potatoes, 3 cooked carrots, ½ seeded cucumber, 2 poached breasts of chicken (about 1½ cups), ¼ pound pre-cooked ham and 2 hard-cooked eggs. All ingredients may be layered into one bowl. Just prior to serving, add one 8-ounce can drained diced beets and toss gently with the following dressing:

(2) *Russian Dressing* Combine ½ cup mayonnaise, ¼ cup dairy sour cream, 2 tablespoons bottled chili sauce, and 1 teaspoon Dijon mustard. Mince and add 1 dill pickle, 1 tablespoon capers, and 2 tablespoons parsley. Stir together and add 1 tablespoon dill weed, 1 teaspoon salt and a little freshly ground black pepper.

Final Preparation Transfer salad to serving dish and decorate the top with an overlapping row of sliced hard-cooked egg.

3 medium boiled potatoes, diced
3 cooked carrots, diced
½ cucumber, seeded and diced
2 breasts of chicken, poached and diced (about 1½ cups)
¼ pound pre-cooked ham,
2 hard-cooked eggs, diced
1 can (8-ounce) diced beets, drained

½ cup mayonnaise
¼ cup dairy sour cream
2 tablespoons bottled chili sauce
1 teaspoon Dijon mustard
1 dill pickle, minced
1 tablespoon capers, minced
2 tablespoons parsley, minced
1 tablespoon dill weed
1 teaspoon salt
Freshly ground black pepper

1 hard-cooked egg, sliced

Deviled Eggs and Caviar

Hard cook 8 eggs. Split lengthwise and remove the yolks. Mash the yolks with 4 tablespoons mayonnaise, 1 tea-

8 hard-cooked eggs, (Page 25)
4 tablespoons mayonnaise
1 teaspoon Dijon mustard

spoon Dijon mustard, 1 tablespoon white wine vinegar, 1 teaspoon salt and a little freshly ground black pepper. Spoon mixture into pastry bag and use to fill whites in rosette pattern. Garnish each with a small amount of black caviar. Arrange on serving dish.

1 tablespoon white wine vinegar
1 teaspoon salt
Freshly ground black pepper
1 jar (2-ounce) black caviar

White Bean Salad

Open and drain two cans (1-pound) Great Northern beans. Rinse under cool running water. Dissolve 1 teaspoon instant chicken bouillon in ¼ cup water in large skillet. Add the beans and heat through. Immediately drain and dress with 4 tablespoons each olive oil and lemon juice, 1 teaspoon ground coriander* and 2 tablespoons each finely minced green onion and parsley. Taste and add salt and pepper as necessary. Serve at room temperature.

*COOK'S TIP: Substitute 2 tablespoons fresh, minced coriander for the ground coriander, if available. (Coriander is also known as Cilantro or Chinese Parsley.)

2 cans (1-pound) Great Northern beans
1 teaspoon instant chicken bouillon
¼ cup water
4 tabespoons olive oil
4 tablespoons lemon juice
1 teaspoon ground coriander*
2 tablespoons minced green onion
2 tablespoons minced parsley
Salt and pepper

Cucumbers in Sour Cream

Peel 3 medium cucumbers, split lengthwise and scoop out the seeds. Slice into ⅛-inch crescents. Sprinkle with salt and let stand until serving time. Blot dry and combine with the following dressing:

3 medium cucumbers
Salt

Sour Cream Dressing Combine ½ cup dairy sour cream, 1 teaspoon dill weed, and 2 tablespoons each finely minced parsley and green onion.

½ cup dairy sour cream
1 teaspoon dill weed
2 tablespoons minced parsley
2 tablespoons minced green onion

Mrs. Conlin's Best Borsch

Advance Preparation (1) *First Day* Heat 2 tablespoons vegetable oil in large kettle and brown a 5-pound chuck roast on all sides. Add a few marrow bones and boiling water to cover. Return to boil and skim surface. Chop and add 1 carrot, 1 rib celery, 1 large onion and several sprigs parsley. Add 1 tablespoon salt, ½ teaspoon black pepper and 2 teaspoons dill weed. Reduce heat to simmer and cook 2 hours. Refrigerate overnight.

2 tablespoons vegetable oil
5-pound chuck roast
A few marrow bones
1 carrot, chopped
1 rib celery, chopped
1 large onion, chopped
Several sprigs parsley, chopped
1 tablespoon salt
½ teaspoon black pepper
2 teaspoons dill weed

(2) *Second Day* Remove solidified fat. Lift out meat and pick over, removing bone, fat and gristle. Cut meat into bite-sized pieces. Strain broth. Return meat and strained broth to kettle. Add one can (1-pound 14-ounce) tomatoes, 4 tablespoons lemon juice, 2 tablespoons sugar and 2 pressed cloves garlic. Bring to simmer and cook 1 hour.

1 can (1-pound 14-ounce) tomatoes
4 tablespoons lemon juice
2 tablespoons sugar
2 cloves garlic, pressed

Final Preparation Fifteen minutes before serving, add 2 cups chopped cabbage and the contents of two 1-pound jars Harvard beets. Taste and add dill, lemon juice or sugar as necessary to sharpen flavor. Transfer to soup tureen. As each serving is ladled into bowls, add a tablespoon of dairy sour cream. Serve with Pirozhky.

2 cups cabbage, chopped
2 jars (1-pound) Harvard beets
1 carton (12-ounce) dairy sour cream

Pirozhky (Meat Filled Turnovers)

(1) *Filling* Sauté one small, minced onion in 2 tablespoons butter until soft. Add ½ pound finely ground chuck and cook until meat loses color. Add ¼ cup double-strength beef bouillon, 1 teaspoon dill weed, ½ teaspoon salt and ¼ teaspoon black pepper. Continue to cook until liquid is absorbed. Cool mixture and add 1 beaten egg.

(2) *Assembly* Cut 3-inch squares from contents of 2 packages refrigerated crescent dinner rolls. Place small amount of filling on each and fold corner to corner to make triangles. Moisten edges and press together with tines of a fork to seal. Place on lightly oiled baking sheet. Bake at 350 degrees for 15 minutes, turning once. Makes 16.

*Pirozhky also make a great appetizer.

1 small onon, minced
2 tablespoons butter
½ pound ground chuck
¼ cup double-strength beef bouillon
1 teaspoon dill weed
½ teaspoon salt
¼ teaspoon black pepper
1 egg, beaten

2 packages refrigerated crescent dinner rolls

Sultana Cake

To be baked 3 days ahead.

(1) Soak 4 cups sultana raisins* in warm water to cover, while preparing cake batter.

(2) Cream together 1 pound butter and 2 cups sugar. Add 6 eggs one at a time, beating well after each addition. Blend in 1 tablespoon rum and ¾ cup milk.

(3) Sift and measure 4½ cups all-purpose flour. Add 1 tablespoon baking powder and 1 teaspoon salt. Sift

4 cups sultana raisins*

1 pound butter
2 cups sugar
6 eggs
1 tablespoon rum
¾ cup milk

4½ cups all-purpose flour
1 tablespoon baking powder
1 teaspoon salt

flour mixture over creamed mixture and blend well.

(4) Drain and blot raisins with paper towels. Toss the raisins with a little flour and fold them into batter. Chop ½ pound citron into fine dice. Toss with a little flour and fold into batter.

½ pound citron

(5) Grease and flour a 10-inch tube or bundt pan. Fill with batter to within ½ inch of top. (If there is extra batter, bake in small loaf pan.) Bake 1 hour and 30 minutes at 325 degrees. Cool in pan 10 minutes. Invert on rack and finish cooling. Remove from pan. Wrap in aluminum foil and let stand at least 3 days before serving. Keeps well for several weeks. Dust with confectioners' sugar before serving.

2 tablespoons confectioners' sugar

*Cook's Tip: Sultana raisins are made from white grapes which are grown in Australia. They are available in foreign countries and larger U. S. cities. If you must substitute in this recipe, use 2 cup golden raisins and 2 cups currants.

Indonesian Pork Sates
Lamb Curry
Chutney and Assorted Condiments
Aromatic Rice Pilau
Puris
Cinnamon-Fried Bananas with Apricot Yoghurt

Beer

The most remarkable single fact about Indian curries is that we don't find them more often on American tables. This menu, which features a fine lamb curry with all the trimmings, may help alter that condition.

A fine accompaniment for cocktails might simply be toasted nuts sprinkled with a mild curry powder. Gin drinks, or cocktails mixed with fresh citrus juice, will set the stage for the highly seasoned curry to follow. An unusual first course of Indonesian Pork Sates can be served in the living room before guests are seated for dinner.

In Indian and other "curry cuisines," you will find some main dishes of curry which contain only vegetables and others that are predominantly meat. You might also find the same vegetables, fruits, nuts and spices both in the curry itself and in the rice. This version of curry includes lamb, fresh vegetables and fruits, while nuts, currants and raisins are added to the rice. The curry is served with a selection of condiments, the most important of which is chutney. All of the flavors are planned to complement each other and there is no real star of the menu. It all goes together.

You will be delighted to know that you can successfully make the remarkable puffed bread known as puris. Though I am hard put to explain why it puffs, it could not be more perfect to serve with curry. The best beverage to serve with curry is either tea or beer.

Collecting the ingredients and preparing this great curry dinner is in itself a lot of fun. Even more fun awaits the creative hostess who enjoys special effect decorating. Just contemplating the designs in a favorite Indian print can stimulate your imagination. You will be inspired to use lots of brass, candlesticks, teak, baskets, incense burners, tropical fruit, and, as the king of Siam was prone to say, "et cetera, et cetera, et cetera."

Indonesian Pork Sates

Advance Preparation (1) *Marinade*
Combine 2 medium chopped onions, 1 clove pressed garlic, ½ teaspoon ground coriander, ½ teaspoon ground

2 medium onions, chopped
1 clove garlic, pressed
½ teaspoon ground coriander
½ teaspoon ground cumin

cumin, 1 teaspoon salt, ¼ teaspoon black pepper, dash cayenne, juice of ½ lemon, 1 tablespoon brown sugar, and 2 tablespoons soy sauce.

(2) Cut 1 pound lean pork into ½-inch cubes. Thread cubes of pork onto 5-inch skewers. Lay skewers in low container. Cover with marinade. Let stand 1 hour.

Final Preparaton Broil skewered pork, 6 inches from broiler or over charcoal, for 8 to 10 minutes. Turn and baste with marinade once during cooking. Arrange on attractive tray and serve in the living room.

1 teaspoon salt
¼ teaspoon black pepper
Dash cayenne
Juice of one-half lemon
1 tablespoon brown sugar
2 tablespoons soy sauce
1 pound lean pork
1 package 5-inch wooden skewers

Lamb Curry

Advance Preparation (1) *Lamb* Cut a 4-pound leg of lamb into 1-inch cubes.

4-pound leg of lamb

(2) *Preparing the Curry* Heat 2 tablespoons oil and 2 tablespoons butter in heavy skillet and brown the cubes of lamb on all sides. Do not allow pieces to touch while browning. (You may have to brown a few pieces at a time.) Stir in 2 tablespoons prepared blended curry powder and continue cooking a minute or two. Add 1 pressed clove garlic, 3 medium chopped onions, 2 ribs chopped celery, and 2 pared and chopped tart apples. Add 1 chopped tomato and 1 small eggplant, pared and cut into ½-inch dice. When all ingredients are heated through, add 2 cups condensed chicken broth. Add 2 teaspoons salt,

2 tablespoons oil
2 tablespoons butter
2 tablespoons curry powder
1 clove garlic, pressed
3 medium onions, chopped
2 ribs celery, chopped
2 tart apples, pared and chopped
1 tomato, chopped
1 small eggplant, pared and cut into ½-inch dice
2 cups canned condensed chicken broth
2 teaspoons salt
2 tablespoons brown sugar
Grated rind from 2 lemons
½ cup yoghurt

2 tablespoons brown sugar and the grated rind from 2 lemons. Stir in ½ cup yoghurt. Cover and simmer 45 minutes. (This dish matures if made the day before and reheated before serving.)

Final Preparation Spread ¾ cup shredded coconut on a baking sheet and toast in a hot oven until golden brown. Reserve. Mince green onion to make ½ cup. Cut 3 or 4 dilled cucumber pickles into uniform ⅛-inch dice. Steam ½ cup dark raisins until plump. Reserve. Dice ½ pound bacon and fry over moderate heat until crisp. Drain on paper towels. Reserve. Place each of the above ingredients in individual bowls. Fill one bowl with ready-made chutney, such as Major Grey's. Transfer Lamb Curry to heated serving dish. Arrange the smaller condiment bowls around Lamb Curry and allow guests to select their favorites.

¾ cup shredded coconut, toasted
½ cup minced green onion
3 or 4 dill pickles, diced
½ cup dark raisins, plumped
½ pound bacon, diced and fried
1 cup ready-made chutney

Aromatic Rice Pilau

Advance Preparation (1) *Aromatic Bouillon* Bring 4 cups water to a boil. Add 4 cloves, 1 stick cinnamon, ⅛ teaspoon powdered saffron and 4 chicken bouillon cubes. Turn off heat and allow to steep for 20 minutes.

(2) *Rice* Melt ¼ cup butter in a heavy kettle and sauté 2 cups converted rice until well coated with butter and turning slightly translucent. Add the Aromatic Bouillon, cover tightly

4 cups water
4 cloves
1 stick cinnamon
1/8 teaspoon powdered saffron
4 chicken bouillon cubes

¼ cup butter
2 cups converted rice

and simmer 15 to 18 minutes or until all liquid is absorbed.

(3) *Additions* Meanwhile, sauté ½ cup slivered almonds, ¼ cup golden raisins and ¼ cup currants in 1 tablespoon butter until almonds are lightly browned.

Final Preparation Stir almonds and raisins into rice. Butter a 6-cup mold, (loaf pan or decorative mold) and pack the hot rice into mold. Invert mold immediately onto a serving platter. Holding the mold firmly against platter, pick up the platter and give it a little jolt against the counter.

COOK'S TIP: I use a brass tray for this rice. The food is not harmed by contact with brass, if it is to be served right away.

½ cup slivered almonds
¼ cup golden raisins
¼ cup currants
1 tablespoon butter

Butter for mold

Puris

Advance Preparation (1) Combine 1-2/3 cups unsifted whole wheat flour with 2-2/3 cups sifted all-purpose flour. Add 2 teaspoons salt. Stir 2 tablespoons vegetable oil into 1¼ cups water and add to flour. Stir to blend well. Shape dough into ball and place on a floured board. Cover with kitchen towel and let stand 30 minutes.

Final Preparation (1) Knead the dough for about 4 minutes or until smooth. Divide into two parts and roll out to a thickness of ⅛ inch. Using a 3-inch English muffin cutter, cut into rounds.

1-2/3 cups whole wheat flour, unsifted
2-2/3 cups all-purpose flour, sifted
2 teaspoons salt
2 tablespoons vegetable oil
1¼ cups water

(2) Heat vegetable oil, in sufficient amount for deep frying, to a temperature of 365 degrees.

Drop the rounds into hot oil until puffed, then turn and continue frying on other side one minute. Remove to paper towels. Serve warm with Lamb Curry. (If made ahead, Puris may be rewarmed in the oven.)

COOK'S TIP: You don't have to use a thermometer for this, but a thermometer would save guessing. If the oil is hot enough the Puris will puff within 30 seconds. If the oil is too hot the Puris will not puff properly. Regulate heat accordingly.

1 quart vegetable oil

Cinnamon-Fried Bananas with Apricot Yoghurt

(1) Peel and slice 4 or 5 bananas on the diagonal. Heat 2 tablespoons butter in skillet. Add the bananas. Combine ½ teaspoon cinnamon with 2 tablespoons granulated sugar. Sprinkle over bananas. Toss gently and cook until bananas are heated through and sugar has caramelized. Spoon into dessert dishes.

(2) Spoon apricot yoghurt, to cover, over warm bananas.

4 or 5 bananas
2 tablespoons butter
½ teaspoon cinnamon
2 tablespoons granulated sugar

2 cartons (8-ounce) apricot yoghurt

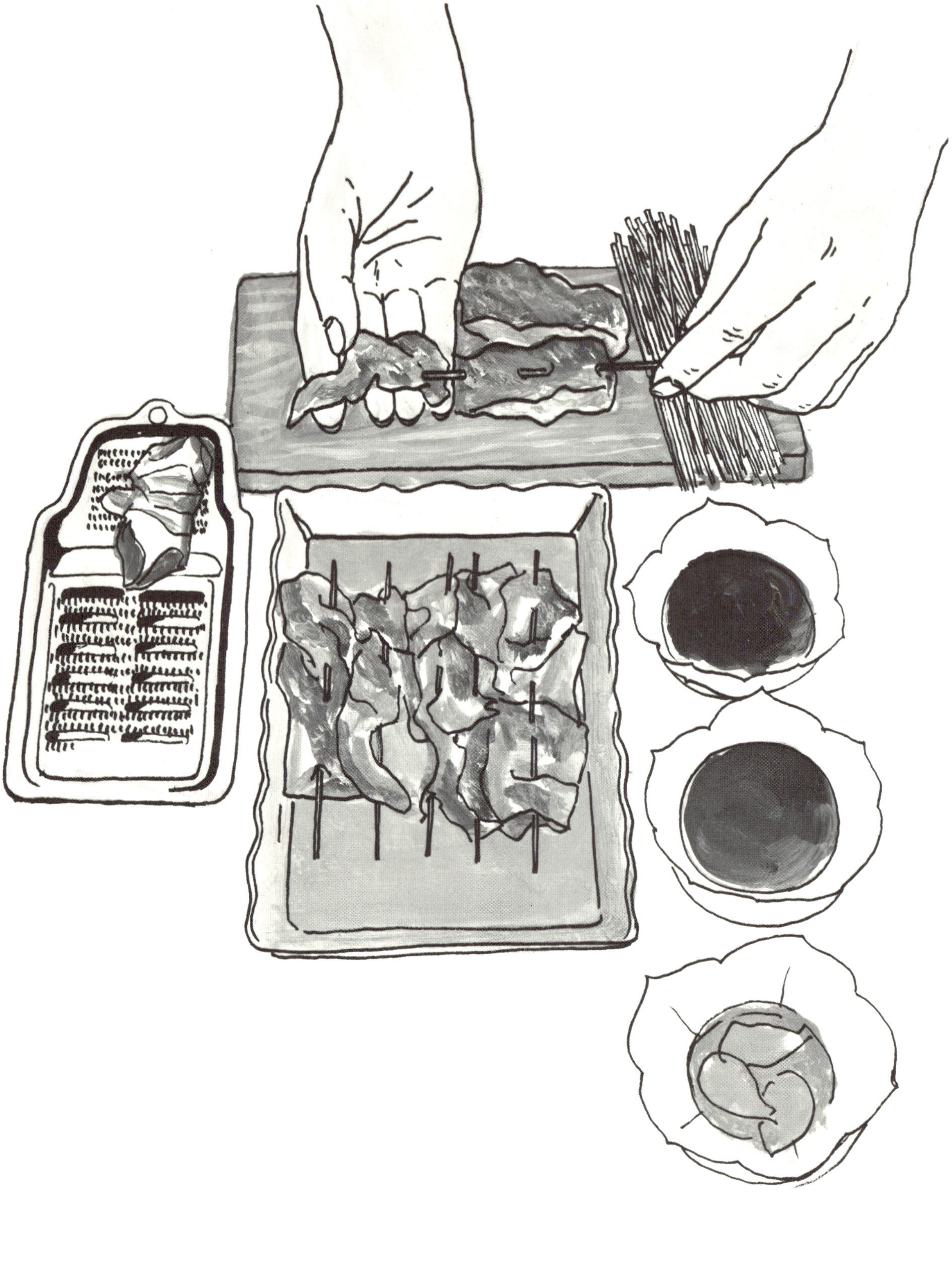

V LOTUS BOWL IMPORTS

The cuisines of the Orient. Four easy-to-master menus of Chinese and Japanese origin. If you never learn to cook anything else "Oriental," you can ride on the reputation created by these.

*Avocado Egg-Flower Soup
Sukiyaki
Steamed Rice
Cucumbers in Rice Wine Vinegar
Green Tea Sherbet
or
Ice Cream with Ginger Marmalade*

Mosel

This menu, featuring sukiyaki, appeals to the hostess who doesn't like to leave her guests when it's time to cook. Sukiyaki is traditionally cooked at the table and until recent years, this was done on a hibachi pot. In modern Japan, single burner electric units have replaced the hibachi, often in partnership with cast-iron utensils. Japanese cooks feel that cooking in iron produces even heat and influences both the flavor and nutritional value of a dish. If you subscribe to this school, your mother's hand-me-down cast iron skillet could be just the thing for cooking sukiyaki. An electric frypan is also very handy for table-top cooking, and is often used to make sukiyaki in American homes.

After the ingredients for sukiyaki have been prepared, they are attractively arranged on a large platter. As much time is given to the artistry of these arrangements as is given to the cooking. This preparation can be done before the guests arrive, and the soy-seasoned cooking stock can also be mixed and waiting in a heat proof pitcher.

After guests are seated, the hostess can proceed with making sukiyaki right at the table. The skillet is heated and the thinly sliced beef and various vegetables are added in layers. A final layer of spinach on top acts as a cover for the dish. The warmed stock is poured over the ingredients and they are allowed to simmer gently until tender crisp. Remember, unlike "stir-frying" in Chinese cooking, the ingredients for sukiyaki are layered into the skillet in a given order and are not disturbed while cooking. It is also important to note that in Japanese cooking, the pan juices are not thickened with cornstarch as they often are in Chinese cooking.

During the few minutes it takes for sukiyaki to cook, you might find your guests silently and expectantly "watching-the-pot." To keep them happily occupied while waiting, serve your first course, avocado egg-flower soup.

With the sukiyaki you will be serving plain steamed rice. A special salad made with cucumbers and rice wine vinegar is planned to follow the main course. Green tea or warm *sake* is traditionally served with Japanese food. On some occasions you might enjoy serving wine with these foods. I like a light and delicate white wine from the Mosel region of Germany.

For dessert I have included a "collector" recipe for green tea sherbet. It was developed in the 1930s by Japanese chefs for the San Francisco World's Fair. Today it can be found only occasionally in Japanese restaurants. There is also an alternate dessert suggestion for ice cream with ginger marmalade. Either dessert should be well received and produces an ideal final flavor for this menu.

Avocado Egg-Flower Soup

Advance Preparation (1) Bring 4 cups condensed chicken broth to a boil. Add 1 teaspoon grated fresh ginger and 1/8 teaspoon granulated garlic.*
(2) Stirring the simmering broth with a fork, gradually pour in 2 lightly beaten eggs. Remove from heat when egg is set.
(3) Peel and slice 2 ripe avocados into long, thin slivers. Place slices in bottom of soup tureen and toss gently with 1 tablespoon lemon juice. Pour the hot chicken broth over avocados. Sprinkle the top with 2 tablespoons minced green onion.

*Cook's Tip: Granulated garlic is available in Oriental import stores. It makes accurate mesaurements possible when cooking small portions.

- 4 cups condensed chicken broth (3 cans [10½-ounce] condensed chicken broth, plus water to equal 4 cups)
- 1 teaspoon grated fresh ginger (Page 93)
- 1/8 teaspoon granulated garlic*
- 2 eggs, lightly beaten
- 2 avocados
- 1 tablespoon lemon juice
- 2 tablespoons finely minced green onion

Sukiyaki (Beef and Vegetables in Bouillon)

Advance Preparation (1) *Beef* Have 1½ pounds beef tenderloin or top sirloin cut about 1 inch thick. Partially freeze and slice into 1/8-inch strips. Arrange on platter.
(2) *Vegetables* As each vegetable is prepared arrange it next to sliced beef on the platter. Cut 2 Spanish onions into 3/8-inch rings. Cut 6 to 8 green onions into 2-inch lengths and split. Cut 3 ribs of celery into long, thin oblique slivers. Wash and trim 8 ounces of fresh mushrooms, and slice

- 1½ pounds beef tenderloin, or top sirloin

- 2 Spanish onions
- 6 to 8 green onions
- 3 ribs celery
- 8 ounces fresh mushrooms
- ½ pound fresh spinach

from stem through cap. Wash and stem ½ pound fresh spinach.

(3) *Saifun (bean thread) Noodles* Simmer 2 to 3 ounces of bean thread noodles in water to cover about 5 minutes. Drain, cool, and arrange on platter.

(4) *Canned Additions* Open and drain 1 can ToFu (bean curd). Cut into ½-inch cubes. Drain 1 can Sheritaki noodles. Arrange these items on platter with other ingredients.

(5) *Soy-Seasoned Cooking Liquid* Combine in saucepan, one can condensed chicken broth plus enough water to make 1½ cups, ¼ cup dry white wine, ½ cup soy sauce and ¼ cup sugar.

Final Preparation Heat a cast iron Dutch oven, iron sukiyaki pan, or electric skillet. Rub bottom with a chunk of suet on a fork, or add 2 tablespoons peanut oil. Fry beef briefly until it has lost most of its color. In the order in which they were prepared, lay all vegetables, except spinach, on top of beef. Add bean thread noodles, bean curd and Sheritaki noodles. Last of all, place spinach leaves on top. Heat the Soy-Seasoned Cooking Liquid and pour over ingredients. When mixture bubbles, lower heat and simmer, uncovered, 10 minutes. Remove from heat and serve in warmed sukiyaki plates, or large plates with a substantial lip on outside edge. Serve with steamed white rice.

2-3 ounces Saifun (bean thread) noodles

1 can (11-ounce, drained weight) ToFu (bean curd)
1 can (8½-ounce) Sheritaki, drained

1 can (10½-ounce) condensed chicken broth, plus water to make 1½ cups
¼ cup dry white wine
½ cup soy sauce
¼ cup sugar

Piece of suet or 2 tablespoons peanut oil

Steamed Rice

(1) Wash 1 cup each long grain and short grain rice in several changes of water. Place the rice in a heavy kettle and add 3 cups cold water. Cover tightly and let stand 1 hour.

(2) Place rice pot on stove and cook over intense heat until water boils. Slip an asbestos mat under pot and when water returns to a boil, lower heat to lowest setting. Cook (by timer) 15 minutes. Do not peek. Remove from heat and let stand 10 minutes before opening pot.

1 cup long grain rice
1 cup short grain rice
3 cups water

Cucumbers in Rice Wine Vinegar

(1) Wash and slice 2 medium cucumbers as thinly as possible. Sprinkle lightly with salt and let stand ½ hour. Blot dry with paper toweling, and combine with dressing below.

(2) Combine ½ cup rice wine vinegar, 2 tablespoons sugar, 1 teaspoon salt and ½ teaspoon MSG (optional). Add to cucumbers and refrigerate until serving time.

(3) *Service* Cucumbers may be served floating in dressing in lotus bowls, or drained and placed on leaves of Bibb or Boston lettuce. If you choose the latter methods, garnish each serving with thinly-sliced red radish.

2 medium cucumbers
Salt

½ cup rice wine vinegar
2 tablespoons sugar
1 teaspoon salt
½ teaspoon MSG (optional)

Optional Service: Bibb or Boston lettuce and thinly-sliced red radish

Green Tea Sherbet

(1) Combine 2/3 cup sugar and 2/3 cup water and boil 5 minutes. Re-

2/3 cup sugar
2/3 cup water

move from heat. Dissolve 1 envelope unflavored gelatin in 2 tablespoons cold water and stir into hot syrup. Add 4 tablespoons lemon juice.

(2) Place 1 heaping teaspoon powdered green tea (Japanese Ceremonial Tea, also known as Matcha) in large mixer bowl. Add 1/3 cup boiling water and beat until frothy. Add syrup from above and 1 cup whole milk. Continue beating only to blend.

(3) Place mixture (still in the bowl) in freezer. When half frozen, remove sherbet from freezer and beat 4 to 5 minutes or until smooth and creamy. Transfer to a covered container and freeze until needed.

(4) At serving time, spoon sherbet into stemmed dessert dishes or lotus bowls.

COOK'S TIP: This recipe for Green Tea Sherbet is a "collector" item. An alternate dessert suggestion follows.

1 envelope unflavored gelatin, dissolved in 2 tablespoons cold water
4 tablespoons lemon juice
1 heaping teaspoon powdered green tea
1/3 cup boiling water
1 cup whole milk

Ice Cream with Ginger Marmalade

Advance Preparation Heat 1 teaspoon oil in small saucepan. Add ¼ cup slivered almonds and toss until lightly browned. Stir in 1 cup ginger marmalade or preserves. Heat until smooth. Remove from heat and stir in 2 tablespoons brandy.

Service For each serving, place a scoop of vanilla ice cream in a small lotus bowl. Top with about 2 tablespoons warm ginger marmalade.

1 teaspoon oil
¼ cup slivered almonds
1 cup ginger marmalade or preserves
2 tablespoons brandy

8 scoops vanilla ice cream

COOK'S TIP: Ginger is a rhizome of a tropical flowering plant. Its spicy flavor can be found in dishes throughout the Oriental menu.

Forms of ginger that can be used in soup and main-dish cooking are the whole dried ginger root, ground ginger, bottled juice, or fresh ginger root. Fresh ginger can be used grated, crushed, or sliced. It can be kept indefinitely if frozen, and grated without being thawed.

To flavor desserts, forms of ginger that may be used are either candied or crystalized, and either preserves or marmalade.

Beef Teriyaki on Skewers
Shrimp and Assorted Vegetables Tempura
Steamed Rice
Lychees and Melon in Japanese Plum Wine

Niersteiner

One of the best inventions of the Japanese cuisine is teriyaki cooking. It employs a marvelous marinade made of soy sauce, sugar, garlic and ginger, and is used in the same way that Westerners use barbecue sauce. It may be used to season meat, poultry or seafoods which are cooked over charcoal. It imparts a pungent, delicate sweetness to foods. As an hors-d'oeuvre for this menu, thin slices of beef are threaded onto skewers and cooked in the teriyaki style. These may be charcoaled by your guests over hibachi pots, or these succulent morsels can be prepared in the kitchen.

A charming Japanese custom which you can adopt to advantage is the use of hot hand towels to follow courses such as this. Brightly-colored fingertip towels of terry cloth are lovely for this purpose. Tightly rolled, the towels are submerged in hot scented water. Squeeze them to remove excess water and present them in an interesting lacquered box, or on a tray.

Another Japanese specialty, which is sure to become one of your favorites, is tempura. The best tempura batter is made from a simple mixture of flour, eggs, and water. It is combined with a light hand, leaving the flour lumpy and not completely dissolved. The most popular item for tempura is shrimp. Together with a variety of vegetables, the shrimp are dipped in batter and deep fried until delicately browned. The best utensil to use is a tempura fryer. They are available as pans for stove-top use, or as electric units. Tempura is served with plain steamed rice and a soy-based dipping sauce.

Chinese and Japanese rice is prepared by a technique well worth incorporating into your repertoire of cooking skills. You begin with plain white, raw rice. This must be rice that has been husked and polished only. Rice that has been processed beyond this point (converted) cannot be successfully cooked by this method. It will take restraint on the part of the cook, as the cover must not be lifted during the entire cooking time, nor for ten minutes afterwards. Rice cooked in this way holds together and is easy to eat with chopsticks.

A simple fruit dessert containing canned lychees and melon balls makes a fine ending for this elegant menu. The fruits are marinated in Japanese plum wine. Japanese plum wine also makes an interesting apertif to precede a menu such as this.

Beef Teriyaki on Skewers (Beef in Japanese Barbecue Sauce)

Advance Preparation (1) *Flank Steak* Remove fat and membrane from a 1½ to 2-pound flank steak and partially freeze. Partially frozen meat is easier to slice.) Slice diagonally across

1½ to 2 pounds flank steak
1 package (7-inch) bamboo skewers

the grain into thin ⅛-inch slices. Strips will be 5 to 6 inches long and from 1 to 1½ inches wide. Take the first strip and accordion-fold it into ¾-inch folds. Run a skewer through the middle of fold, then straighten the meat by pulling each end of the strip toward the ends of the skewer. Skewer the remaining strips in this way. Line skewers up in rows in flat container and pour the marinade over them. Marinate 30 minutes.*

*COOK'S TIP: When preparing skewered beef teriyaki for a crowd, the container can be covered at this point and placed in the freezer. On the day of the party, remove from freezer about 4 hours before cooking time. Turn in marinade while thawing.

(2) *Marinade* Combine ½ cup dry white wine, ¾ cup soy sauce, 1/3 cup brown sugar, 1 tablespoon dry sherry and 1 tablespoon grated fresh ginger.

½ cup dry white wine
¾ cup soy sauce
1/3 cup brown sugar
1 tablespoon dry sherry
1 tablespoon grated fresh ginger

Final Preparation To Cook Skewered meat can be cooked by guests over charcoal in a hibachi pot for 1 to 2 minutes on each side. To prepare by frying, drain slices and lay in hot oiled skillet, turning once, just until meat loses color. Serve at once.

Tempura (Batter Coated Shrimp and Vegetables, Deep Fried)

Advance Preparation (1) *Tempura Dipping Sauce* Combine ¼ cup soy sauce, ½ cup condensed beef bouil-

¼ cup soy sauce
½ cup condensed beef bouillon

lon, 1 tablespoon dry white wine, 1 tablespoon sugar, and 1 tablespoon grated fresh ginger. Place in a saucepan and reserve until serving time.
Service At serving time heat the sauce and serve warm in individual dipping bowls beside each plate. (The tiniest lotus bowls are perfect.)
(2) *Preparation of Tempura Ingredients Shrimp* Wash 24 jumbo shrimp in salted water and drain. Remove all shell except tail section. Cut off the very back tip of tails in a straight line. Slit back of shrimp almost through to underside and remove vein. Flatten shrimp with handle of knife into butterfly. Reserve.
Carrots Pare 4 or 5 carrots and cut on the oblique into long, thin slices.
Onions Peel two medium Spanish onions and cut into 3⁄8-inch rings. Separate rings, discarding the very center of each slice.
Parsley Select 2 uniform full-leafed sprigs of parsley per serving.
(3) *Tempura Batter* Add 1 egg to 1½ cups cold water and beat lightly. Add 1½ cups flour and stir in, leaving some flour undissolved.

COOK'S TIP: Tempura batter mix is available in Oriental import stores and is well worth seeking out.

Final Preparation Add peanut oil to tempura fryer (or utensil of similar purpose) to a depth of 2½ to 3 inches. Heat to approximately 350 degrees. Holding shrimp by tail section,

1 tablespoon dry white wine
1 tablespoon sugar
1 tablespoon grated fresh ginger

24 jumbo green shrimp
Salted water

4 or 5 carrots

2 medium Spanish onions

2 bunches parsley (to make 16 sprigs)
1 egg
1½ cups cold water
1½ cups flour

1 quart peanut oil

dip into batter and drop into hot oil. Turn once or twice and cook a total of 3 to 4 minutes. Drain on paper towels and place on heated serving platter in warm (lowest setting) oven. Proceed with frying remaining ingredients by dipping first in batter, then into hot oil; carrots, onions and parsley, in that order. The batter should be light golden in color when items are cooked. Serve with dipping sauce and steamed rice.

Steamed Rice
Prepare 1 recipe Steamed Rice by directions on Page 91.

1 recipe Steamed Rice (Page 91)

Lychees and Melon in Japanese Plum Wine
Open and drain one 1-pound can whole seedless lychees. Thaw, but do not drain, 2 packages frozen melon balls. Combine the two and add ¾ cup white Japanese plum wine. Serve in lotus bowls, with ready-made Hapi Ginger Folds or other dessert cookie as desired.

1 can (1-pound) whole seedless lychees
2 packages (10-ounce) frozen melon balls
¾ cup white Japanese plum wine
1 package (4-ounce) Hapi Ginger Fold cookies

Chinese Shrimp Toast and Plum Sauce
Rock Cornish Hens Teriyaki
Pork Fried Rice
Celestial Chicken Salad
Oriental Fruits in Gingered Honey

Vouvray, demi-sec

This is an eclectic menu featuring specialties of both the Chinese and Japanese cuisines. We begin with a delectable Chinese hors-d'oeuvres of shrimp toast which contains many of the ingredients found in egg rolls. These ingredients are spread on triangles of bread and deep-fried. Quite remarkably everything holds together for this procedure. When you serve shrimp toast from an attractive laquered tray, with little bowls of plum sauce and hot mustard, you can enjoy all of the exquisite qualities of egg rolls without the work of making them.

Next, a Japanese teriyaki dish featuring rock Cornish hens. This delectable little bird, whether served whole or split, makes very attractive portions to be served in an Oriental menu. Its size is in keeping with the tradition of eating light amounts of meat and poultry. The teriyaki method of cooking renders rock Cornish hens more flavorful than when cooked by more ordinary methods.

One of the most useful techniques you can incorporate into everyday cooking practice is that of frying rice in the Chinese manner. It is a marvelous way to use leftover rice, as the rice used should be *cold,* and preferably day-old. One delicious version of this dish, pork fried rice, accompanies the Cornish hens in this menu. Once you have mastered it, use your imagination to create new and different combinations as leftovers become available in your refrigerator.

Celestial salad is made from shredded lettuce, slivered cold chicken, and fried bean thread noodles. The bean thread noodles give the salad an unusual texture. Salt, pepper, and a traditional Chinese seasoning known as "spice powder" are used in conjunction with toasted sesame seeds and almonds to produce a unique "dry dressing" for the salad. It can be served as a separate course, or it can accompany other dishes on the menu.

Both Chinese and Japanese desserts are problematical for the average homemaker. The pastries are rather complicated and contain ingredients such as bean paste, which stops most Western cooks before they begin. There are other excellent desserts which contain rice, but we hesitate to repeat rice in the dessert if it has been served with the main dishes. The best solution is to use fresh or canned fruit which originate in tropical climes. Flavored with ingredients native to the cuisines of the Orient, fruit desserts such as the one presented here, can be outstanding.

Shrimp Toast

Advance Preparation (1) Mince and combine ½ pound raw shrimp, 3 green onions and 6 water chestnuts. Add 2 tablespoons soy sauce, 1 teaspoon salt, 1 teaspoon grated fresh ginger, 1 teaspoon sesame oil (optional), 2 tablespoons cornstarch and 1 beaten egg.
(2) Trim crusts from 10 slices white sandwich bread. Cut each slice into 4 triangles.
Final Preparation At serving time spread shrimp mixture on bread triangles and drop into hot (350 degrees) peanut oil. Turn once, remove and drain on paper towels. Arrange Shrimp Toast on a serving tray with small bowls of Chinese Plum Sauce and Chinese Hot Mustard for dipping.

½ pound raw shrimp, minced
3 green onions, minced
6 water chestnuts, minced
2 tablespoons soy sauce
1 teaspoon salt
1 teaspoon grated fresh ginger
1 teaspoon sesame oil, optional
2 tablespoons cornstarch
1 egg, beaten
10 slices white sandwich bread

Peanut oil, sufficient for deep-frying
1 small jar ready-made plum sauce (or sweet and sour sauce)
Chinese Hot Mustard, bottled, or homemade (directions for making on container)

Rock Cornish Hens Teriyaki (Japanese-Style Barbecued Cornish Hens)

Advance Preparation (1) *Rock Cornish Hens* Select 4 (1-pound) Cornish hens and split them in half. Wash and pat dry. Marinate in Teriyaki Sauce for 3 to 4 hours, refrigerated.
(2) *Teriyaki Sauce* Combine 1/3 cup

4 (1-pound) Cornish hens

1/3 cup soy sauce

soy sauce, 2 tablespoons sugar, 3 tablespoons sherry or Mirin and 1 tablespoon grated fresh ginger.

Final Preparation Preheat oven to 375 degrees. Place Cornish hens on a rack, leaving space between, and roast about 50 minutes. Turn and baste with marinade, once or twice while baking. When done, place hens on a heated serving platter and garnish platter with sprigs of watercress and several preserved kumquats placed at random.

2 tablespoons sugar
3 tablespoons sherry or Mirin
1 tablespoon grated fresh ginger

1 bunch watercress, washed and crisped
Several preserved kumquats

Pork Fried Rice

(1) Heat 2 tablespoons peanut oil in a wok or heavy skillet. Beat 4 eggs with 1 tablespoon water and add to hot oil. Cook as for scrambled eggs. Remove eggs and chop into small pieces.

2 tablespoons peanut oil
4 eggs, beaten with 1 tablespoon water

(2) Add 2 tablespoons additional peanut oil to wok or skillet and fry 1 cup of slivered lean pork. Open and drain 1 can bean sprouts and add to pork. When heated through, add 3 cups cold (preferably day-old) cooked white rice.

2 tablespoons peanut oil
1 cup slivered lean pork
1 can (1-pound) bean sprouts, drained
3 cups cold cooked rice

(3) Return the eggs to rice mixture and toss constantly while adding 3 to 4 tablespoons soy sauce. When rice is heated through, remove from heat. Scatter ½ cup minced green onions over top. Cover and keep warm until serving time.

3 to 4 tablespoons soy sauce
½ cup minced green onion

Celestial Chicken Salad

Advance Preparation (1) *Breast of Chicken* Poach a double breast of chicken in water to cover, with a slice of fresh ginger and ⅛ teaspoon Chinese Spice Powder.* When tender, remove and chill. Cut into slivers.

(2) *Seasoning* Combine 1 teaspoon salt, ¼ teaspoon black pepper, and ⅛ teaspoon Chinese Spice Powder.* Place 2 tablespoons sesame seeds in heavy iron skillet and toast over high heat. Stir into salt mixture. Add ½ teaspoon peanut oil to skillet and toast ¼ cup slivered almonds. Reserve.

*Cook's Tip: Chinese Spice Powder is a blend of five spices which is available in Oriental import stores. It is also known as Chinese cinnamon and *heang fun.*

Final Preparation (1) *Lettuce* Shred (with a stainless steel knife) one-half head iceberg lettuce. Place in mound on large round serving platter. Scatter the slivered breast of chicken over lettuce, and sprinkle with about 1/3 of Seasoning mixture (Step 2).

(2) *Saifun (Bean Thread) Noodles* Take a bundle of bean thread noodles about as big as the inside cardboard roll from a roll of paper towels. Pull the noodles apart gently so as not to break them up. Heat 2 inches peanut oil in tempura fryer. To test temperature of oil, drop a 1-inch length of noodle into oil. It will sink. When it pops to the surface and inflates, then

1 double breast of chicken
Water to cover
1 slice fresh ginger
1/8 teaspoon Chinese Spice Powder*

1 teaspoon salt
¼ teaspoon black pepper
1/8 teaspoon Chinese Spice Powder
2 tablespoons sesame seeds, toasted
½ teaspoon peanut oil
¼ cup slivered almonds

½ head iceberg lettuce
Seasoning (Step 2, Advance Preparation)

1 bundle Saifun (bean thread) noodles
Peanut oil, sufficient for deep-frying

you know that the oil is hot enough. Pick up the whole bundle of bean thread noodles and place it on top of the hot oil. It will immediately puff up like clouds (thus the name Celestial). Handling with tongs, grasp it right in the middle and turn it over exposing the top side of bundle to the hot oil for just one instant. Lifting with tongs, place cloud of noodles on top of lettuce on platter. (If desired, noodles may first be wrapped in a kitchen towel, and crushed gently. This facilitates service somewhat.) While still warm, sprinkle noodles with remaining Seasoning. Garnish the top with toasted slivered almonds.

Toasted slivered almonds (Step 2, Advance Preparation)

Oriental Fruits in Gingered Honey

(1) Combine ¼ cup honey, 2 tablespoons Grand Marnier or other orange-flavored liqueur and 2 tablespoons minced candied ginger.

(2) Open 1 can whole seedless lychees and 1 can whole seedless loquats. Do not drain. Open and drain 1 can defrosted frozen pineapple chunks and 1 can mandarin oranges. Place fruit in your most attractive Oriental style bowl and add the honey-ginger mixture. Marinate 1 to 2 hours.

(3) At serving time, bring serving bowl right to the **table** and spoon fruit and lots of juice into dessert-size lotus bowls.

¼ cup honey
2 tablespoons Grand Marnier
2 tablespoons candied ginger, minced

1 can (1-pound) whole seedless lychees
1 can (1-pound) whole seedless loquats
1 can (12-ounce) frozen pineapple chunks, drained
1 can (12-ounce) mandarin oranges, drained

Chinese Garlic Spareribs
Chicken and Black Mushrooms
Beef and Pea Pods with Oyster Sauce
Sweet and Sour Shrimp
Steamed Rice
Almond Cookies and Tea

Vouvray Balzac

If inserts for fortune cookies contained hints for preparing Chinese food, the messages might read, "He who wishes to cook honorable Chinese dinner, must first get very organized."

Such organization begins with the guest list. Cooking a Chinese dinner means that more than eight people would be considered a crowd. A solo cook cannot comfortably produce enough food for more and also enjoy the party. The amount of food included in a dish is never doubled or tripled to accommodate a larger group, but rather another dish is added to the menu as the guest list grows.

The second step of organization will be concerned with assembling ingredients. Many people complain that their home-cooked Chinese food is never as good as it is in restaurants. If this is true, not enough attention has been given to securing the authentic ingredients which produce an authentic taste. Seek out foreign markets which feature imported foods, and cut substitutions to a minimum.

All of these recipes are divided into two major steps of preparation. In *advance preparation* you will pare, peel, and slice all ingredients. As each item is made ready for cooking, it is placed on a separate dish. The dishes are arranged in order of use, as you will find that ingredients are added to the wok or frypan one at a time and often in rapid succession. This advance preparation can spell the difference between success and failure, and should be complete before your guests arrive.

In the *final preparation* you will do the actual cooking. Most Chinese dishes can be fully cooked in less than five minutes. The greatness of these dishes is lost completely if you try to "make-ahead-and-reheat" them. Since the cooking time is minimal, if you understand the method and have everything arranged in the order that it is to be used, you will be surprised to learn how very simple Chinese cooking actually is.

This is a beautiful menu which will produce authentic flavors throughout, and establish your reputation as a fine cook. The foods can either be served in courses or placed on the table together in banquet fashion. Tea may be served throughout the menu, or, if you prefer to serve wine, you will be very impressed with Vouvray Balzac.

Chinese Garlic Spareribs

(1) Have 2 pounds tiny lean spareribs cut into 1½-inch lengths. Place on a rack in a 350-degree oven and roast 1 hour.

(2) *The Sauce* Combine ¼ cup soy sauce, ¼ cup red wine vinegar, 1 cup brown sugar, 1 teaspoon each dry mustard and grated fresh ginger and 2 pressed cloves garlic. Cook mixture in skillet or wok for 3 to 5 minutes.

(3) Add precooked spareribs. Continue cooking and tossing until ribs are coated with the caramelized sauce. Serve at once. Or finish to this point. Reheat in a 350-degree oven.

2 pounds tiny lean spareribs, cut into 1½-inch lengths

¼ cup soy sauce
¼ cup red wine vinegar
1 cup brown sugar
1 teaspoon dry mustard
1 teaspoon grated fresh ginger
2 garlic cloves, pressed

Chicken and Black Mushrooms

(1) *Advance Preparation* Cut 3 double chicken breasts into uniform 1½-inch strips. Discard bone and connecting tissues. Sprinkle with 1 tablespoon dry sherry.

3 double chicken breasts
1 tablespoon dry sherry

(2) Slice 12 to 16 water chestnuts. Drain one can bamboo shoots. Crush 10 to 12 black beans and soak in 2 tablespoons water. Soak 10 to 12 black mushrooms (Chinese dried) in warm water.

Final Preparation Heat 3 tablespoons peanut oil in skillet and add ½ teaspoon each salt and MSG.* Add slivered chicken and stir-fry 2 to 3 minutes. Add, one at a time: bamboo shoots and black beans (with water), and water chestnuts. Heat through after each addition. Add drained black mushrooms last and add ½ cup condensed chicken broth at that time. Allow to come to a simmer and add 1 teaspoon cornstarch dissolved in 1 teaspoon cold water. Continue cooking until sauce is clear and smooth.

*COOK'S TIP: Often in Chinese cookery you are instructed to add the seasoning ingredients, such as salt, MSG and ginger, to the hot *oil* before the addition of remaining ingredients. This is because *oil* has the curious quality of carrying flavor evenly throughout foods with which it is combined.

12 to 16 water chestnuts
1 can (6-ounce) bamboo shoots
10 to 12 black beans (tow-shee)
2 tablespoons water
10 to 12 black mushrooms (Chinese dried)
3 tablespoons peanut oil
½ teaspoon salt
½ teaspoon MSG, optional
½ cup condensed chicken broth
1 teaspoon cornstarch, dissolved in 1 teaspoon cold water

Beef and Pea Pods in Oyster Sauce

(1) *Advance Preparation* Cut 1 pound top sirloin or beef tenderloin into ⅛-inch slices. Combine 2 tablespoons dry sherry, 2 tablespoons soy sauce, 4 teaspoons cornstarch, 1 tea-

1 pound top sirloin, or beef tenderloin
2 tablespoons dry sherry
2 tablespoons soy sauce
4 teaspoons cornstarch

spoon grated fresh ginger, ¼ teaspoon granulated garlic and ½ teaspoon MSG. Stir into beef and marinate until cooking time.
(2) Wash and remove woody ends from stems of ¼ pound white mushrooms. Slice from stem through cap. Wash and string 8 ounces snow peas.
(3) *At Serving Time* Place 3 tablespoons peanut oil in skillet and heat. Add beef and stir-fry until meat loses color. Add mushrooms and cook 2 minutes. Combine 1 cup condensed chicken broth, 1 teaspoon sugar and 4 tablespoons oyster sauce. Add to beef and simmer 1 to 2 minutes. Combine 1 teaspoon cornstarch dissolved in 1 teaspoon water. Add to sauce and cook until clear and smooth. Add pea pods and cook no longer than 1 minute. Transfer to heated serving dish.

1 teaspoon grated fresh ginger
¼ teaspoon granulated garlic
½ teaspoon MSG

¼ pound white mushrooms
8 ounces snow peas (pea pods)
3 tablespoons peanut oil
Sliced beef (Step 1)
Mushrooms (Step 2)
1 cup condensed chicken broth
1 teaspoon sugar
4 tablespoons oyster sauce
Snow peas (Step 2)
1 teaspoon cornstarch, dissolved in 1 teaspoon water

Sweet and Sour Shrimp

Advance Preparation (1) Sprinkle 1 pound peeled and deveined raw shrimp with salt and dust lightly with flour.
(2) Make thin Tempura Batter by recipe on Page 96. Dip shrimp in batter and fry in hot peanut oil just until batter is set *(Stage-frying).**
Drain on paper towels and reserve.

*Cook's Tip: *Stage-frying* is a method used in Chinese cookery to facilitate quick and easy final preparation; getting as much done ahead as possi-

1 pound peeled deveined raw shrimp
Salt
Flour
1 recipe Tempura Batter (Page 96)
2 cups peanut oil

ble, you might say.

(3) *The Sauce* Combine in saucepan one can (20-ounce) pineapple chunks, 1 cup water, 1 teaspoon grated fresh ginger, 3 tablespoons brown sugar, 1 tablespoon soy sauce and ¼ cup white vinegar. Simmer gently 5 to 8 minutes. Cut a carrot into flowerettes* and drop into sauce. Thicken sauce with 2 tablespoons cornstarch dissolved in 2 tablespoons cold water. Add a green bell pepper cut into 1-inch cubes. Turn off heat. Do not cover.

*COOK'S TIP: Carrot flowerettes may be made by scoring the surface of the carrot in several parallel lines lengthwise, with either a knife tip or a lemon-zester. Then cut the carrot horizontally into very thin slices.

Final Preparation and Serving Reheat oil and refry shrimp until golden. Transfer to heated serving platter. Reheat sauce and spoon over shrimp. Garnish top with ½ cup Gwa Ying (Sweet Cucumber) or Preserved Mixed Vegetables.

- *1 can (20-ounce) pineapple chunks*
- *1 cup water*
- *1 teaspoon grated fresh ginger*
- *3 tablespoons brown sugar*
- *1 tablespoon soy sauce*
- *¼ cup white vinegar*
- *1 carrot*
- *2 tablespoons cornstarch dissolved in 2 tablespoons cold water*
- *1 green bell pepper*

- *½ cup Gwa Ying (Sweet Cucumber) or Preserved Mixed Vegetables*

Steamed Rice

Prepare one recipe Steamed Rice by directions on Page 91.

- *1 recipe Steamed Rice (Page 91)*

Almond Cookies

Cream together 1 cup sugar, ¾ cup butter, 1 egg, 1 tablespoon water, 4

- *1 cup sugar*
- *¾ cup butter*

ounces almond paste and a drop of yellow food coloring. Sift and measure 2 cups all-purpose flour. Add 1 teaspoon baking powder and a pinch of salt. Add to creamed mixture. Roll cookie dough into 1-inch balls and place on greased baking sheet. Flatten cookies with thumb and press a whole blanched almond into each. Bake at 350 degrees for 12 to 15 minutes, or until lightly browned.

1 egg
1 tablespoon water
4 ounces almond paste
1 drop yellow food coloring
2 cups all-purpose flour
1 teaspoon baking powder
Pinch of salt
6-ounce package whole blanched almonds

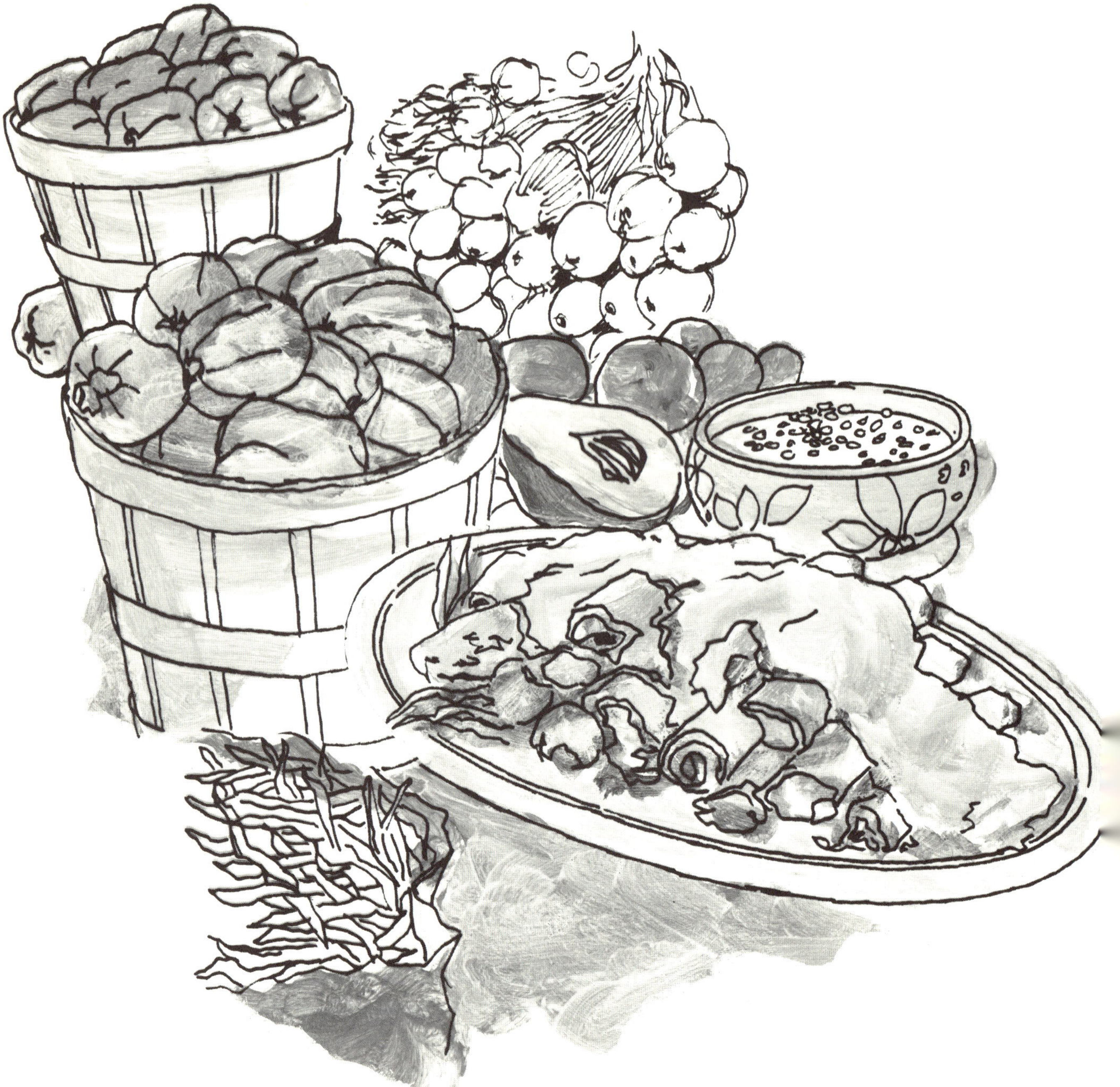

VI Amigos de Mexico

For friends of Mexico who like a little vim and vigor in what they eat. A unique cuisine created from foods native to the southwestern United States and northern Mexico.

White Wine Sangria
Huevos Rancheros
Melon and Tropical Fruit Platter

Sangria, the renowned wine punch of Spain, is also popular in Mexico. For morning parties, you will find that it produces a pleasant transition between waking up and feeling sociable. Although Sangria is usually made from red wine, this white wine version is more suitable for many menus.

Several countries have a traditional breakfast of almost "national" proportions. In the United States, of course, it's bacon and eggs. In France, it's croissants and café au lait. In Holland, it's cold meats and cheeses, assorted breads, and a soft-boiled egg. In Mexico, it's huevos rancheros, or ranch-style eggs.

Every province of Mexico has its own version of huevos rancheros, the sauce for which varies with the type of green chilis that are available in each locale. This recipe is typical and it is mild enough for most palates.

The peasant bread of Mexico, tortillas, can be made from corn or wheat flour. Corn flour tortillas are by far the more common. For huevos rancheros, tortillas are fried until crisp and topped with fried eggs and a highly seasoned tomato sauce. The sauce is made with canned *Tomatoes and Green Chilis,* a product which is available today in most supermarkets.

If it is possible to do so, purchase fresh tortillas when you are planning to cook Mexican food. If you must buy frozen tortillas, which are now available in most supermarkets, you can render them much more palatable by letting them thaw completely. Then warm them directly on the open burner, either gas or electric at moderate heat. Flip them over repeatedly from side to side until warm and dry. After this, proceed with recipe as if using fresh tortillas.

The platter of tropical fruits presented here can serve as a colorful table decoration as well as a refreshing and satisfying final flavor. Place it in the center of your table while dining. For dessert, bring out fresh plates and allow your guests to choose fruit or melon, as desired.

White Wine Sangria

(1) Combine ½ cup water, 1 cup sugar, and ¼ teaspoon ground cinnamon or one cinnamon stick. Bring to simmer and cook 5 minutes. Slice one lemon, one orange and one banana. Pour hot syrup over fruit and refrigerate.

(2) At serving time, transfer fruit mixture to a large clear glass pitcher. Add 2 bottles dry white wine, such as a California Mountain Burgundy. Add a tray of ice cubes and stir. Serve in wine glasses.

½ cup water
1 cup sugar
¼ teaspoon ground cinnamon or 1 stick of cinnamon
1 lemon
1 orange
1 banana
2 bottles dry white wine
1 tray ice cubes

COOK'S TIP: You may substitute dry red wine for white wine in this recipe. In addition to fruits listed here, you may use peaches, nectarines or strawberries.

Huevos Rancheros
(Ranch-Style Fried Eggs)

Advance Preparation (1) *The Sauce* Sauté 2 medium chopped onions and 2 pressed cloves garlic in 3 tablespoons olive oil until limp. Stir in 2 cans Tomatoes and Green Chilis. Add 1 teaspoon ground cumin and 1 teaspoon salt. Simmer 10 minutes.
(2) *Tortillas* Heat ½ inch vegetable oil in heavy pan. Fry tortillas one at a time until crisp and lightly browned on both sides. Drain on paper towels.
Final Preparation Fry eggs in butter as to individual preference for fried eggs. As each is finished, place it on top of prepared tortilla and spoon ranchero sauce to cover over each. This allows 4 single and 4 double servings.

2 medium onions, chopped
2 cloves garlic, pressed
3 tablespoons olive oil
2 cans (10-ounce) Tomatoes and Green Chilis
1 teaspoon ground cumin
1 teaspoon salt

1 cup vegetable oil
1 dozen tortillas

1 dozen eggs
Butter, for frying eggs

COOK'S TIP: If you wish to expand this menu, you may add 1 recipe Guacamole and 1 recipe Refried Beans. Place servings on same plate with Huevos Rancheros.

Optional: 1 recipe Guacamole (Page 117), and 1 recipe Refried Beans (Page 118)

Melon and Tropical Fruit Platter

(1) Place a whole fresh pineapple upright in center of a large round Tray. Remove peeling from an additional

2 fresh pineapples

pineapple. Cut into quarters, remove core, and slice into triangular serving pieces.

(2) Peel, seed and quarter watermelon, cantaloupe and honeydew melon. Cut quarters into triangular serving pieces.

(3) Arrange pineapple and melon pieces spoke-fashion around base of pineapple. Fill in with canned mandarin oranges and fresh Thompson seedless grapes.

(4) *Service* Use this tray as a centerpiece during meal. When dinner plates are removed, bring out dessert plates and allow guests to serve themselves.

1 small watermelon
1 cantaloupe
1 honeydew melon

1 can (15-ounce) mandarin oranges
2 pounds Thompson seedless grapes

Seviche
Soft Chicken Tacos   Tostadas Con Frijoles
Spiced Pumpkin Flan

Beer

Seviche, an excellent seafood cocktail of South American origin, is a great first course for Mexican and other summer menus. Fresh fish, shrimp, or scallops are usually cooked only by the acidity of fresh lime juice. This recipe for Seviche utilizes frozen seafood. It is best when it is just briefly simmered in a spicy citrus marinade, then chilled several hours.

Tacos are as popular in Mexico as hamburgers are in America. The best known tacos are made from folded and fried-until-crisp tortillas, which are then filled with meats and salad greens. *Soft* tacos are also served along the Mexican border. I think you will find the soft chicken tacos included here much to your liking. In this version, "soft-fried" tortillas are filled with beautifully seasoned minced chicken and garnished with guacamole.

Another much loved specialty found along the border is Tostadas con Frijoles, sometimes called Chalupas. These tostadas are made by spreading crisply fried tortillas with refried beans and shredded cheese. Just prior to serving, they are baked until the cheese is melted and lightly browned. They are served topped with a big mound of chopped lettuce and tomatoes. For a light repast, two or three tostadas can be served alone. When served alone, they are made a little more hearty by the addition of slivered left-over turkey, chicken or roasted meats.

Flan, that marvelous egg custard which is baked in its own caramel sauce, is a favorite dessert of all who come to know it. The flan presented here is extra-special, as it contains pumpkin and delicate spices. It can be made well ahead and unmolded just prior to serving time.

To decorate for your Mexican menus, bring forth all the souvenirs that have come your way. Or, look in specialty shops for inexpensive decorations such as piñatas, paper flowers, or colorful pieces of pottery. Try a still-life arrangement around a guitar, or combine sombreros, strings of painted gourds and candles. Brightly colored burlap or striped awning material could provide an interesting background or tablecloth.

Seviche (Raw Fish Appetizer)

Advance Preparation (1) *The Fish* Thaw, in the package, 2 pounds frozen filets of sole.* (Overnight in the refrigerator will do nicely.)

2 pounds filets of sole, frozen or fresh

*COOK'S TIP: When fresh sole is available, proceed with recipe omitting Step 3, as the fish will be adequately cooked in the *fresh* lime and orange juice.

Cut sole into ½-inch cubes and lay in bottom of enameled pan. Sprinkle

1 teaspoon salt
Dash Tabasco

with 1 teaspoon salt and a dash Tabasco.

(2) *Additions* Add 4 sliced green onions, one thinly sliced red onion, 1 clove pressed garlic, ½ teaspoon oregano, 1 bay leaf and 1 tablespoon white wine vinegar. Add ½ cup each *fresh* lime juice and orange juice.

(3) Place over heat and bring to simmer, turning gently. Remove from heat. Cover and chill several hours.

Final Preparation* Serve Seviche, including poaching liquid, in scallop shells or icers with salted cocktail crackers or tortilla chips.

4 green onions, sliced
1 red onion, thinly sliced
1 clove garlic, pressed
½ teaspoon oregano
1 bay leaf
1 tablespoon white wine vinegar
½ cup fresh lime juice
½ cup fresh orange juice

Salted cocktail crackers, or tortilla chips

*Cook's Tip: When avocado is not being used elsewhere in the menu, cut 2 avocados into ¼-inch cubes, toss with lemon juice and fold into Seviche just prior to serving — great!

Soft Chicken Tacos
(Minced Chicken in Fried Tortillas)

Advance Preparation (1) Place one 3-pound frying chicken in water to cover, with a Vegetable-Herb Bouquet, Page 170. Simmer until tender. Remove and cool. Remove meat from bones and return skin and bones to stock pot. Mince the chicken meat and reserve for filling. Continue simmering stock until reduced to one cup; strain and reserve for sauce.

(2) *Sauce* Sauté one minced green onion in 2 tablespoons olive oil. Stir in 2 tablespoons flour and ½ teaspoon each salt, ground cumin and

1 (3-pound) frying chicken
Water to cover
Vegetable-Herb Bouquet (Page 170)

1 green onion, minced
2 tablespoons olive oil
2 tablespoons flour
½ teaspoon salt

ground coriander. Add a pinch white pepper and a grating of nutmeg. Add one cup chicken stock (Step 1), and one 3-ounce package cream cheese. Stir until thick and smooth.

(3) *Filling* Combine sauce with minced chicken meat (Step 1).

(4) *Tortillas* Fry 16 tortillas on both sides in ½ inch vegetable oil until lightly browned but still pliable. Fold in half and drain on paper towels.

(5) *Guacamole* Peel and seed 2 ripe avocados. Mash with a fork. Add 2 finely diced ripe tomatoes, 2 minced green onions, 2 tablespoons lemon juice, and 2 to 4 tablespoons olive oil. Add ¼ teaspoon paprika and ½ teaspoon salt. Stir all together to blend.

Final Preparation Place about 3 tablespoons chicken filling in fold of each tortilla. As tortillas are filled, arrange them in overlapping rows on ovenproof platter. Just prior to serving, heat tacos in a 350-degree oven for 10 to 12 minutes. Remove from oven and spoon a ribbon of Guacamole down center of each row.

COOK'S TIP: To test avocados for ripeness, press gently. The surface should give a little, but there should be no remaining indentation. Ripe avocados can be held without further ripening for one or two days if refrigerated. To force ripening, wrap avocados in newspapers and put them in a warm place (around 80 degrees) overnight.

½ teaspoon ground cumin
½ teaspoon ground coriander
A pinch white pepper (1/8 teaspoon)
A grating of nutmeg (1/8 teaspoon)
1 cup chicken stock (Step 1)
1 package (3-ounce) cream cheese

16 tortillas
Vegetable oil for deep frying

2 avocadoes, mashed
2 tomatoes, finely diced
2 green onions, minced
2 tablespoons lemon juice
2 to 4 tablespoons olive oil
¼ teaspoon paprika
½ teaspoon salt

Filling from Step 3
Tortillas from Step 4
Guacamole from Step 5

Tostadas Con Frijoles
(Toasted Crisp Tortillas with Beans)

Advance Preparation (1) *Refried Beans* Sauté one chopped onion and one clove pressed garlic in 2 tablespoons olive oil in a cast iron skillet. Stir in one can refried beans and bake in the skillet for 20 minutes in a 350-degree oven.

1 medium onion, chopped
1 clove garlic, pressed
2 tablespoons olive oil
1 can (1-pound) refried beans

(2) *Cheese* Shred and reserve ½ pound mild cheddar or Monterrey Jack cheese.

½ pound mild cheddar or Monterrey Jack cheese

(3) *Salad Topping* Combine ½ head shredded lettuce, 2 diced tomatoes, 2 minced green onions and one sliced avocado. (Sprinkle sliced avocado with lemon juice to prevent darkening.) Add salt to taste to salad mixture.

½ head lettuce, shredded
2 tomatoes, diced
2 green onions, minced
1 avocado, sliced
2 tablespoons lemon juice
Salt to taste

(4) *Tortillas* Heat ½ inch vegetable oil in skillet and fry 8 tortillas, turning once, until crisp and lightly browned. Drain on paper towels.

8 tortillas
½ cup vegetable oil

Final Preparation Spread each tortilla with Refried Beans, sprinkle with shredded cheese and place on baking sheet. Bake at 350 degrees for 12 minutes or until cheese is melted. Remove from oven and top each serving with a mound of Salad Topping. Serve at once with bottled green taco sauce, if desired.

Bottled green taco sauce, optional

Spiced Pumpkin Flan

Advance Preparation (1) Place 1 cup granulated sugar in a cast iron skillet and stir with a wooden spoon over

1 cup granulated sugar

moderate heat until sugar has melted and turned golden. Pour into a 4 or 6-cup charlotte mold or bread loaf pan. Turn to coat inside of mold with caramel.

(2) Beat together 4 eggs, ½ cup sugar, ¼ teaspoon salt, 1 teaspoon vanilla, 2 teaspoons pumpkin pie spice, 1 can (15-ounce) pumpkin and 1-2/3 cups evaporated milk.

(3) Pour mixture into prepared mold. Place mold in a shallow pan of hot water and bake at 350 degrees for 1½ hours or until a knife blade can be inserted and withdrawn clean. Cool and refrigerate until serving time.

Final Preparation and Service Run tip of knife around top of flan and invert on serving dish. Add 2 tablespoons water to caramel remaining in mold. Place mold in 200-degree oven until caramel is dissolved. Pour over flan. Cut into wedges and spoon a little caramel sauce over each serving.

4 eggs
½ cup sugar
¼ teaspoon salt
1 teaspoon vanilla
2 teaspoons pumpkin pie spice
1 can (15-ounce) pumpkin
1-2/3 cups evaporated milk

Chili con Queso and Tostadas
Mexican Green Peppers and Salsa De Tomate
Arroz Blanco
Ensalada Con Guacamole
Ice Cream with Rum-Currant Sauce

Beer

Along the Texas border of Mexico, a colorful and flavorful cuisine has developed which is lovingly called "Tex-Mex." It is composed of ingredients which are native to the arid plains of northern Mexico and the rich soil of the lower Rio Grande Valley of Texas. Residents of the area have been nurtured since childhood on the flavors of Spanish onions, garlic, jalapeños, avocados, and a divine elixir from south of the border known as *rum*.

A popular dish found on holiday tables and at summer cook-outs as well is Chili con Queso. This could also be called Mexican fondue, as it is a chafing dish presentation of melted cheese which is highly seasoned with green chilis and tomatoes. Chili con Queso is eaten with toasted tortilla chips and it can be served as either an appetizer to precede a variety of "Tex-Mex" menus, or on its own as a snack.

Driving along farm-to-market roads in the Rio Grande Valley, you will see acres of luscious green bell peppers growing in the fields. On Valley tables, you will find these peppers filled with spicy mixtures of meat, raisins and nuts. They are baked in a richly flavored tomato sauce, or sometimes encased in a light batter and deep-fried. The baked version is included here, served with plain white rice.

Avocados are also grown along the Mexican border. In this menu, avocado is added to Sauce Vinaigrette and tossed with salad greens, for an unusually good summer salad.

Scoops of cinnamon, chocolate and coffee ice cream are arranged in alternating layers in a pretty serving bowl, then glazed with rum-flavored currant sauce. This dessert provides a cool, pleasurable contrast to the spiciness of the entrée.

Chili Con Queso and Tostados
(Melted Cheese and Peppers with Crisp Tortillas)

(1) Sauté 1 medium chopped onion and 2 cloves pressed garlic in 2 tablespoons olive oil until limp. Stir in 1½ tablespoons flour. Add 1 can Tomatoes and Green Chilis and simmer until thickened. Stir in ½ pound shredded Monterrey Jack cheese. Stir until melted and smooth.

1 medium onion, chopped
2 cloves garlic, pressed
2 tablespoons olive oil
1½ tablespoons flour
1 can (10-ounce) Tomatoes and Green Chilis
½ pound Monterrey Jack cheese

(2) Transfer mixture to candle-warmer serving dish and keep warm while serving. Serve with tostadas (quartered tortillas *fried-until-crisp*) or packaged tortilla chips.

1 dozen tortillas, quartered and fried, or 1 package tortilla chips

Mexican Green Peppers con Salsa De Tomate (Green Peppers with Tomato Sauce)

Advance Preparation (1) *Green Pepper Cases* Cut the tops from eight small, uniform green bell peppers. Carefully remove seeds and membrane. Drop into boiling salted water and simmer, uncovered, about 3 minutes. Remove peppers and turn upside down to drain.

8 small green bell peppers
Boiling salted water

(2) *Meat Filling* Sauté 1 large minced onion and 2 cloves pressed garlic in 2 tablespoons olive oil until cooked but not brown. Add 1 pound ground chuck and continue to cook while adding a grating of nutmeg, and 1 teaspoon each ground cumin, salt and chili powder. Soak 1 cup seasoned bread stuffing mix in ½ cup bouillon and stir into meat mixture. Add ½ cup raisins and ¼ cup slivered almonds. Remove from heat and stir in 2 beaten eggs.

1 large onion, minced
2 cloves garlic, pressed
2 tablespoons olive oil
1 pound ground chuck
A grating of nutmeg (1/8 teaspoon)
1 teaspoon ground cumin
1 teaspoon salt
1 teaspoon chili powder
1 cup seasoned bread stuffing mix
½ cup bouillon
½ cup raisins
¼ cup slivered almonds
2 eggs, beaten

(3) *Salsa de Tomate* Sauté 1 medium chopped onion and 2 cloves pressed garlic in 2 tablespoons olive oil. When soft, add one can tomato sauce, ½ cup water, 1 teaspoon each ground cumin and chili powder, ½ teaspoon ground coriander and a grating of nut-

1 medium onion, chopped
2 cloves garlic, pressed
2 tablespoons olive oil
1 can (8-ounce) tomato sauce
½ cup water

meg. Simmer 10 minutes.

Final Preparation Fill green pepper cases with Meat Filling and place in greased baking dish. Spoon Salsa de Tomate over peppers.* Cover dish and bake for 45 minutes at 350 degrees. Remove cover and continue baking 10 or 15 minutes. Serve with Arroz Blanco (plain white rice).

*Cook's Tip: This dish can be frozen at this point. To cook, thaw completely and proceed with baking directions.

1 teaspoon ground cumin
1 teaspoon chili powder
½ teaspoon ground coriander
A grating of nutmeg (1/8 teaspoon)

Arroz Blanco (White Rice)

Prepare 1 cup converted rice by package directions.

1 cup converted rice

Ensalada con Guacamole (Green Salad with Avocado Dressing)

Advance Preparation (1) Wash and prepare 2 or 3 salad greens. Roll greens in kitchen towels and refrigerate until needed. Peel and cut one red onion into thin slices and separate rings. Cut two tomatoes into wedges and sprinkle with salt. Reserve.
(2) *Guacamole Salad Dressing.* Peel and seed one avocado. Mash with a fork. Add 1 minced green onion, 1 tablespoon lemon juice and 2 tablespoons olive oil. Stir to blend. Add ⅛ teaspoon paprika and ¼ teaspoon salt. Combine with ½ cup Sauce Vinaigrette aux Fines Herbes.
Final Preparation and Service Break salad greens into chilled bowl. Add

2 or 3 selected salad greens (Page 29)
1 red onion, thinly sliced
2 tomatoes

1 avocado
1 green onion, minced
1 tablespoon lemon juice
2 tablespoons olive oil
1/8 teaspoon paprika
¼ teaspoon salt
½ cup Sauce Vinaigrette aux Fines Herbes (Page 24)

red onion rings and tomato wedges. Spoon Guacamole Dressing over salad and toss gently with a rolling motion.

Ice Cream with Rum-Currant Sauce

(1) Make small, uniform balls of ice cream from cinnamon, chocolate and coffee ice cream, allowing 2 per person. Wrap balls individually in plastic wrap and keep in freezer.

1 pint cinnamon ice cream
1 pint chocolate ice cream
1 pint coffee ice cream

(2) *Rum-Currant Sauce* Pour boiling water to cover over ½ cup currants and allow to plump. Drain and add 2 tablespoons dark Jamaican rum. Marinate until needed. Combine ¾ cup brown sugar and 1 tablespoon cornstarch in saucepan. Add 1 cup boiling water and cook until clear. Stir in 2 tablespoons butter and a dash each salt and nutmeg. Stir in currants and rum. Cool.

Boiling water
½ cup currants
2 tablespoons dark Jamaican rum
¾ cup brown sugar
1 tablespoon cornstarch
1 cup boiling water
2 tablespoons butter
A dash salt
A grating of nutmeg (1/8 teaspoon)

Final Preparation At serving time, unwrap ice cream balls and place in glass serving bowl, alternating flavors. Pour the Rum-Currant Sauce over ice cream balls and allow guests to choose favorite flavors.

COOK'S TIP: If there is any ice cream left in serving dish, stir it until marbleized. Place in covered container and freeze. Makes an excellent dessert for another day.

Tostadas con Queso
Carne Asada Tampiqueno
Salsa Verde   Refried Beans   Guacamole
Sour Cream Chicken Enchiladas
Mangos on Ice
or
Pineapple-Meringue au Rhum

Sangre de Toro or California Pinot Noir

If the fine hotel chefs of Mexico were invited to submit an "haute cuisine" entry for the international menu, it might well be Carne Asada Tampiqueño. Translated, this means roasted meat in the style of Tampico.

Each of the thirty-two states of Mexico has its own special version of Carne Asada. The Gran Hotel Ancira in Monterrey serves a handsome one. It is beautifully and ceremoniously served from a huge silver platter. Thinly sliced charcoal grilled tenderloin of beef is arranged in the center of the platter. It is surrounded by Guacamole, Refried Beans, and Chicken Enchiladas. The Carne Asada included in this menu is much the same in its final presentation, although it is geared to preparation in the American kitchen.

Most Mexican food goes well with beer, but Carne Asada calls for a fairly robust red wine, such as Sangre de Toro, imported from Spain, or a California Pinot Noir.

A more perfect dessert than fresh mangos would be hard to find. Unfortunately, the season is limited and availability is undependable. Although mangos should be your first choice, an excellent alternate dessert would be pineapple, which also grows abundantly in Mexico. In the recipe included here, servings of pineapple are drizzled with rum and baked with a meringue topping.

I sometimes call this my "black tie" Mexican dinner, as it is served with much formality in Mexico. Your best tablecloth, finest crystal, and tallest candelabra are called for and no extra table decorations are necessary. The food itself provides enough color and atmosphere for a memorable evening.

It would be even more memorable for the ladies if they each found a lovely fresh flower tucked in their napkins — possibly a hibiscus or a sprig of bougainvillea.

Tostadas con Queso
(Crisp Tortillas with Cheese)

Advance Preparation Cut ½ dozen tortillas into quarters. Fry in deep fat until crisp and lightly browned. Drain on paper towels and place on baking sheets. Sprinkle with salt. Scatter generous amounts of shredded mild cheddar cheese on tortillas. Mince 2 tablespoons Roasted and Peeled Green Chilis and scatter at random on top of cheese.

Final Preparation Just prior to serving, place Tostadas in a 375-degree oven and bake 8 to 10 minutes. Transfer to serving dish and pass during cocktail hour.

½ dozen tortillas
Vegetable oil, sufficient for deep-frying
Salt to taste
1 cup mild cheddar cheese, shredded
2 tablespoons Roasted and Peeled Green Chilis, minced

Carne Asada (Mexican Roast Beef)

Advance Preparation (1) *Steaks* Have 8 (¾-inch) steaks cut from the large end of a beef tenderloin. Pound each steak between sheets of waxed paper to a thickness of ½ inch. Split each steak lengthwise to make 16 strips of beef (2 strips per serving). Rub steaks with olive oil and a little freshly ground black pepper. Leave at room temperature for 1 hour before cooking.

(2) Grill steaks for 2 minutes on each side in electric skillet at highest set-

8 steaks (from large end of beef tenderloin)
2 to 4 tablespoons olive oil
Freshly ground black pepper

ting. Or, if convenient, grill them over hot charcoal. Arrange steaks in rows in the center of a large heated platter. Prepare 1 recipe Guacamole and place at one end of platter. Prepare 1 recipe Refried Beans and place at other end of platter. Make rows of Sour Cream Chicken Enchiladas down each side. Spoon a ribbon of Salsa Verde down row of steaks and pass remainder at the table.

(3) *Salsa Verde* Combine ½ cup each minced green pepper, Spanish onion and tomato. Stir in 2 tablespoons Roasted and Peeled Green Chilis, 1 teaspoon ground cumin, 1 pressed clove garlic, ½ teaspoon salt and 2 tablespoons minced cilantro or 1 teaspoon ground coriander.* Just prior to serving, heat sauce and simmer about 5 minutes. Spoon part of Salsa down row of steaks as garnish. Pass remainder at the table.

*See Cook's Tip Page 76.

1 recipe Guacamole (Page 117)
1 recipe Refried Beans (Page 118)

½ cup green pepper, minced
½ cup Spanish onion, minced
½ cup tomato, minced
2 tablespoons Roasted and Peeled Green Chilis
1 teaspoon ground cumin
1 clove garlic, pressed
½ teaspoon salt
*2 tablespoons cilantro, minced or 1 teaspoon ground coriander**

Sour Cream Chicken Enchiladas (Tortillas Filled with Chicken in Sour Cream Sauce)

Advance Preparation (1) *Chicken* Simmer one 3-pound frying chicken until tender, in water to cover, with a Vegetable-Herb Bouquet. When chicken is cool enough to handle, remove meat from bones. Mince the meat and reserve. Return skin and bones to stock pot and continue sim-

1 (3-pound) frying chicken
Vegetable-Herb Bouquet (Page 170)

mering until stock is reduced to 1 cup. Strain and reserve for Sauce.

(2) *Sour Cream Sauce* Sauté 2 minced green onions and 1 pressed clove garlic in 4 tablespoons butter. Stir in 4 tablespoons flour and cook one minute without browning. Add 1 teaspoon each salt and ground cumin, ½ teaspoon ground coriander, ⅛ teaspoon white pepper and a grating of nutmeg. Stir in 1 cup chicken stock (Step 1) and 1 can Tomatitos Verdes, drained to equal 1 cup. Cook until thickened and smooth. Remove from heat and stir in 1 cup dairy sour cream.

(3) *Chicken Filling* Stir ½ cup of Sour Cream Sauce into reserve minced chicken meat.

Final Preparation Reheat vegetable oil from Tostadas con Queso. Soften 16 tortillas in hot oil, one at a time, and blot on paper towels.*

*Cook's Tip: Tortillas will tear if removed from hot oil too soon, but they must *not* be allowed to become crisp. This procedure is necessary to keep tortillas from disintegrating in the baking sauce.

While still warm, fill each tortilla with 3 tablespoons Chicken Filling and roll up. Place enchiladas snug against one another in greased baking dish. Spoon remaining Sour Cream Sauce over enchiladas. Bake at 350 degrees for 30 minutes. Arrange 8 enchiladas in a row on each side of steaks on platter.

2 green onions, minced
1 clove garlic, pressed
4 tablespoons butter
4 tablespoons flour
1 teaspoon salt
1 teaspoon ground cumin
½ teaspoon ground coriander
1/8 teaspoon white pepper
A grating of nutmeg (1/8 teaspoon)
1 cup chicken stock (Step 1)
1 cup (8½-ounces) Tomatitos Verdes
1 cup dairy sour cream

16 tortillas
Vegetable oil, sufficient for deep frying

Chicken Filling, Step 3
Sour Cream Sauce, Step 2

COOK'S TIP: Traditionally, all of these foods are arranged on one platter. However, if space is limited on your platter, you may serve the enchiladas from the baking dish.

Mangos on Ice

Select 8 fresh ripe mangos. Spear the stem end of each mango with a dinner fork so that the seed, which is quite flat, is firmly held between the tines of the fork. On the opposite end of the mango cut through the skin only in several places, to resemble the petals of a flower. Peel the skin back the length of the mango. Leaving the forks in place, lay mangos on beds of crushed ice on individual dessert plates. Holding the mango by the attached fork, it is eaten as one would eat a banana.

8 fresh ripe mangos
8 cups crushed ice

*COOK'S TIP: Since the mango season is limited, use Pineapple-Meringue au Rhum (See below.) as an alternate dessert.

Pineapple-Meringue au Rhum

Advance Preparation (1) Cut 2 fresh ripe pineapples into quarters right through the leaf end, making sure leaves are attached to each serving. Remove core and loosen meat from rind. Cut each serving into bite sizes, but leave the meat in place. Drizzle each serving with 1 teaspoon each dark Jamaican rum and brown sugar.

2 pineapples
1 teaspoon dark Jamaican rum per serving
1 teaspoon brown sugar per serving

Wrap leaves in aluminum foil. Reserve.

(2) *Meringue* Place 4 egg whites in large mixer bowl. Add ¼ teaspoon cream of tartar and a dash of salt. Beat until soft peaks have formed and gradually add ¼ cup granulated sugar. Continue beating until peaks are firm and glossy.

Final Preparation and Service Mound each quarter of pineapple with Meringue and spread to cover completely. Arrange on baking sheets and place in middle of a 350-degree oven. Bake 8 to 10 minutes or until lightly browned. Remove from oven. Remove foil from leaves and serve as soon as possible.

4 egg whites
¼ teaspoon cream of tartar
Dash of salt
¼ cup granulated sugar

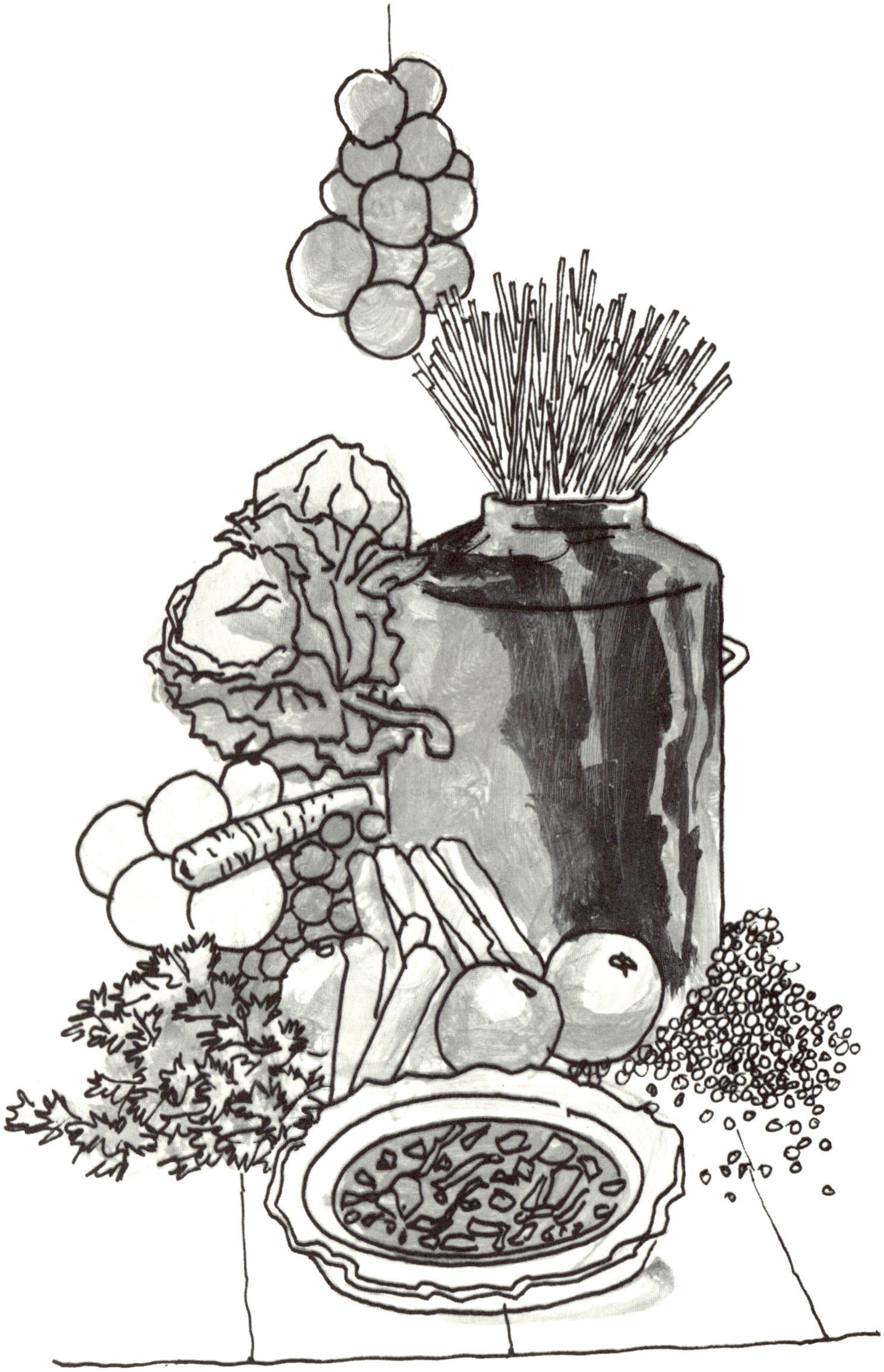

VII BUON GUSTO ITALIANO

"You're invited . . . I'm cooking Italian." That's all you need to say and they'll know it's a party! Unusual Italian specialties, easy to prepare and authentic in every way.

Minestrone with Pesto Sauce
Green Pepper Frittata   Roasted Sweet Sausage
Biscuit Tortoni

Soave

This menu is suggested as a light supper. It would also be good for brunch on a crisp fall day and could easily be expanded for extra guests.

We begin with the popular main-dish soup, minestrone, a hearty soup containing both beans and pasta. Near the end of the cooking time, fresh zucchini and cabbage are added to give the soup additional texture and a quality of freshness. At serving time, this version of minestrone is deliciously accented with the flavor of a unique green sauce known as *pesto*.

Pesto sauce is made from fresh basil, garlic, Parmesan cheese and olive oil blended to a paste with a mortar and pestle. (Thus the name.) It is found on tables along the Mediterranean coasts of both Italy and France, where it is known as *pistou*. In the American kitchen, this marvelous sauce can be turned out in minutes with an electric blender.

If you find yourself intrigued by the notion of making pesto, by all means plan ahead. Make it during summer months when fresh basil is available. Pesto can be frozen and kept all winter, to enhance soups and pastas. Enjoy it as a condiment whenever dining *à l'Italiene*.

For the Italian cooking enthusiast, there is nothing more fun than to seek out and shop in an Italian grocery store. As you walk in, you'll be beset with twinges of hunger while inhaling all the wonderful aromas. The air is permeated with garlic, cheese, sausages, and freshly baked bread. It is an exhilarating experience!

If you've never had Italian sausages, there are two types. One is "hot" and one is "sweet." I find that girls in my cooking class much prefer the sweet. It can be roasted on a rack in the oven and is absolutely delicious! It can, of course, be found in Italian grocery stores, but today it can be found in most supermarkets as well.

In this menu, roasted sweet sausage is served with a green pepper frittata. Frittatas are an Italian version of the omelet. Like the omelet, one is limited only by his imagination as to what can be included in the basic mixture of eggs, garlic, and grated cheese. You might use mushrooms, spinach, asparagus, zucchini, artichoke hearts, parsley and/or herbs, as desired.

The choice for dessert with this menu is Biscuit Tortoni, which is light, interesting, and typically Italian in flavor. Marsala wine, chopped candied fruits, and almond macaroons are suspended in creamy meringue and frozen in paper cups. It can be made days ahead which means this is a handy dessert to serve when entertaining large numbers of people.

Minestrone with Pesto Sauce
(Italian Bean Soup with Basil Sauce)

Advance Preparation (1) *Beans* Soak 2 cups dried white beans (Great Northern or imported Cannellini) in water to cover overnight. Drain, cover with fresh water and bring to boil. Reduce heat and add 2 teaspoons salt and ½ teaspoon freshly ground black pepper. Simmer covered for 1 hour. (2) *Seasoning Ingredients* Meanwhile, sauté in ¼ cup olive oil, 1 cup each chopped celery, onion and carrot. Add 2 cloves pressed garlic. At end of first hour of cooking, add the sautéed vegetables, one large can Italian tomatoes, ¼ cup minced parsley and ½ teaspoon each basil, thyme and crushed bay leaf. Add 2 cans condensed chicken broth. Continue simmering for one hour or until beans are tender.

COOK'S TIP: You may cease cooking at this point, and finish cooking just before serving.

Final Preparation Just prior to serving, add 2 cups shredded cabbage and 2 or 3 sliced zucchini. Stir in 1 cup broken macaroni. Simmer, uncovered, for 15 minutes, stirring occasionally. *To Serve* Ladle into soup bowls and pass the Pesto Sauce (see next page) which is stirred into soup as desired by guests.

2 cups dried white beans
Cold water to cover
2 teaspoons salt
½ teaspoon freshly ground black pepper

¼ cup olive oil
1 cup chopped celery
1 cup chopped onion
1 cup chopped carrot
2 cloves garlic, pressed
1 can (1-pound 14-ounce) Italian tomatoes
¼ cup minced parsley
½ teaspoon basil
½ teaspoon thyme
½ teaspoon crushed bay leaf
2 cans (10½-ounce) condensed chicken broth

2 cups shredded cabbage
2 or 3 zucchini, sliced
1 cup broken macaroni

Pesto Sauce (Basil Sauce)

Combine in top of blender: 2 cups fresh basil leaves (if basil is limited, use 1 cup each fresh basil leaves and parsley stripped from stems), 1 teaspoon salt, ½ teaspoon black pepper, 1 pressed clove garlic and 2 tablespoons pine nuts or walnuts. Add ½ cup Parmesan cheese. As blender runs, pour in ½ cup olive oil gradually, pushing ingredients down and adding more olive oil if necessary to make a smooth paste.

2 cups fresh basil leaves, or 1 cup basil leaves and 1 cup parsley stripped from stems
1 teaspoon salt
½ teaspoon black pepper
1 clove garlic, pressed
2 tablespoons pine nuts or walnuts
½ cup grated Parmesan cheese
½ cup olive oil

Green Pepper Frittata (Italian Baked Omelet with Peppers)

(1) Remove the seeds from 3 medium green peppers and shred fairly fine. Combine with ½ cup chopped green onion and sauté in 2 tablespoons olive oil until limp.

(2) Beat together 10 eggs, 1/3 cup grated Romano cheese, 1 tablespoon minced parsley, 1 teaspoon salt, ¼ teaspoon black pepper and 1 pressed clove garlic. Stir the green pepper mixture into eggs.

(3) Heat 2 tablespoons olive oil in a 9 or 10-inch cast iron skillet. Turn the egg mixture into skillet and cook until set on bottom. Transfer to a 350-degree oven and bake uncovered about 10 minutes or until set on top. Slide onto heated serving plate and cut into wedges to serve.

*Cook's Menu Tip: On some occa-

3 medium green bell peppers
½ cup green onion, chopped
2 tablespoons olive oil

10 eggs
1/3 cup grated Romano cheese
1 tablespoon minced parsley
1 teaspoon salt
¼ teaspoon black pepper
1 clove garlic, pressed
2 tablespoons olive oil

sions you might want to serve Buttered Mushroom-Spaghetti, page 151, with Roasted Sweet Sausage rather than the Frittata.

Roasted Sweet Sausage

Cut 2 pounds Italian sweet sausage into serving pieces. Place on a rack in roasting pan. Fill bottom of roasting pan with ½ inch water. Bake in a 375-degree oven for 30 minutes, turning once or twice.

2 pounds Italian sweet sausage

Biscuit Tortoni (Frozen Cream and Meringue with Fruit)

(1) Marinate ½ cup chopped candied red and green cherries in 2 tablespoons Marsala while preparing remaining ingredients.
(2) Beat 1 cup whipping cream with 3 tablespoons confectioners' sugar until thick and firm.
(3) Add a pinch of cream of tartar to 2 egg whites and beat until frothy. Gradually add 3 tablespoons confectioners' sugar and beat until stiff peaks have formed.
(4) Pulverize enough almond macaroons to make ½ cup crumbs.
(5) Fold all ingredients together and spoon into muffin size foil baking cups. Place filled cups in muffin pans. Sprinkle each with toasted slivered almonds and freeze until needed.

½ cup red and green cherries, chopped
2 tablespoons Marsala wine

1 cup whipping cream
3 tablespoons confectioners' sugar
2 egg whites
Pinch cream of tartar
3 tablespoons confectioners' sugar

½ cup almond macaroon crumbs (Recipe on Page 8)
12 foil baking cups
¼ cup toasted slivered almonds

COOK'S TIP: Marsala is the best known of the Italian fortified wines.

It is a staple ingredient for those who cook lots of Italian food. Some Marsalas are labeled "dry", others "sweet." Actually, they both are fairly sweet. You should buy the "dry" as is can be used in entrées as well as desserts, or it can be sipped as an after-dinner treat.

Garden Relish Antipasto Salad
Lasagne Bolognese   Braised Celery and Zucchini
Toasted Garlic Bread
Macedonia De Frutta Al Marsala

Bardolino

À la Grecque is a method of cooking used along the Mediterranean coasts of Italy and France. It is a method by which a variety of summer vegetables are cooked in a mixture of olive oil, garlic, and herbs resembling a highly seasoned sauce vinaigrette. Cooking is ceased when the vegetables are tender-crisp ("al dente"). They are then marinated in the cooking liquid until they completely absorb all its flavor.

Our first course is an antipasto salad with fresh garden vegetables prepared à la Greque. Ripe olives and pimentos are added and it is served in lettuce cups, garnished with slivers of salami and provolone cheese. This unusual first course salad is a beautiful way to announce that the fine Italian specialties to follow are also out of the ordinary.

Bolognese cooking, the cooking of northern Italy, is becoming more and more familiar to American palates. It is characterized by delicate seasonings, and many dishes are made with *white* sauces rather than the more typical *red* sauces. This menu is built around such a dish, a Bolognese version of lasagne. Basic ingredients are lasagne noodles, Sauce Béchamel, spinach and a flavorful meat sauce made from veal, pork and beef. Discreet amounts of Parmesan cheese are used for flavor, but not so much as to completely sabotage anyone's good intentions about cutting down on calories.

In addition to the fine ingredients included in this basic recipe, you are encouraged to survey the kitchen and use up leftovers. Odds and ends of vegetables such as mushrooms, zucchini, peas, celery or fennel, and roasted meats, leftover turkey or cold chicken, can be added to give the dish a character all its own each time it is made.

With the lasagne you would enjoy either Bardolino or Valpolicella. These are two delightful, light red wines from neighboring vineyards in northern Italy. They go well with most Italian food and are relatively inexpensive, even though imported. They are best when consumed within three to five years.

Fresh summer fruits or quick-thaw frozen fruits marinated in Marsala wine provide a final flavor of authenticity for this menu. Served in stemmed dishes, this is a simple dessert which can change its nationality with the type of wine or liqueur used to flavor it.

For other menus, try the same dessert flavored with Kirsch, Cointreau, Framboise, Vin Rosé, or a favorite fruit wine — whatever transition you need to give the menu a flavor appropriate to the cuisine.

Garden Relish Antipasto Salad (Cooked and Marinated Vegetable Appetizer)

Advance Preparation (1) *Antipasto* The day before needed, pare and trim 4 carrots, ½ head cauliflower, 3 ribs celery and 1 green pepper. Cut the carrots with crinkle cutter into ¼-inch slices on the oblique. Cut cauliflower into flowerettes. Cut celery into 2-inch fingers, and cut pepper into strips, lengthwise.

(2) Combine in a skillet ¾ cup white

4 carrots
½ head cauliflower
3 ribs celery
1 green pepper

¾ cup white wine vinegar

wine vinegar, ½ cup olive oil, 1 teaspoon salt, 2 tablespoons sugar, 1 clove pressed garlic and a little freshly ground black pepper. Bring to simmer and add ingredients from Step 1.

(3) Simmer, with cover ajar, about 8 minutes, stirring once or twice. Remove from heat. Stir in 1 can drained ripe olives and 1 jar pimento, drained and cut into strips. Place Antipasto in covered container and refrigerate overnight. (Good for several days.)
Final Preparation and Service Arrange crisp lettuce leaves on chilled salad plates. Add a scoop of Antipasto and garnish each serving with several strips of salami and provolone cheese. Serve with bread sticks or toasted garlic bread.

½ cup olive oil
1 teaspoon salt
2 tablespoons sugar
1 clove garlic, pressed
Freshly ground black pepper

1 can (7¼-ounce) ripe olives, drained
1 jar (4-ounce) pimento

8 lettuce leaves
½ pound salami, cut into strips
½ pound provolone cheese, cut into strips

Lasagne Bolognese

Advance Preparation (1) *Meat Sauce* Sauté in 2 tablespoons olive oil, ½ cup each finely diced carrot, onion, and celery. When vegetables are cooked through but not brown, stir in ½ pound Italian sweet sausage, removed from casings and broken up. Cook until lightly browned. Add, one at a time, ½ pound each ground round steak, ground lean pork and ground veal, stiring each until it loses its color.*

*Cook's Tip: Some areas have beef, pork, and veal, ground and packaged together for use in meat leaves or

2 tablespoons olive oil
½ cup finely diced carrot
½ cup finely diced onion
½ cup finely diced celery
½ pound Italian sweet sausage
½ pound ground round steak
½ pound ground lean pork
½ pound ground veal

meat balls. Look for it in Packaged Meats, or ask the butcher.

Add ½ cup dry white wine or dry Vermouth. Add ¼ cup tomato paste and 2 cups double-strength beef bouillon. Add 1 tablespoon Spice Islands spaghetti sauce seasoning, 1 teaspoon salt and a little freshly ground black pepper. Cover and simmer about 30 minutes.

(2) *Spinach* Cook one package frozen chopped spinach by package directions and reserve.

(3) *Sauce Béchamel* Prepare 1 recipe Sauce Béchamel by directions on Page 10.

(4) *The Lasagne* To 4 quarts rapidly boiling water add 1 tablespoon each salt and oil. Add 9 strips lasagne, a few at a time. Simmer, uncovered, 15 minutes. Drain and rinse in cold water. Line up on kitchen towels until needed.

(5) *Cheese* Grate and have ready ½ cup Romano or Parmesan cheese.

Final Preparation (1) Butter a 3-quart oblong oven-to-table serving dish. (I like to use my 15-inch copper au gratin pan.) Coat bottom lightly with small amount Meat Sauce. Lay in 3 strips lasagne, overlapping slightly. Add one-third remaining Meat Sauce, and drizzle with one-third Sauce Béchamel. Add one-half of spinach and a little grated cheese.

(2) Add second layer of 3 strips lasagne and repeat Meat Sauce, Sauce

½ cup dry white wine or dry Vermouth
¼ cup tomato paste
2 cups double-strength beef bouillon
1 tablespoon Spice Islands spaghetti sauce seasoning
1 teaspoon salt
Freshly ground black pepper

1 package (10-ounce) frozen chopped spinach

1 recipe Sauce Béchamel (Page 10)

4 quarts boiling water
1 tablespoon salt
1 tablespoon oil
9 strips lasagne

½ cup grated Romano or Parmesan cheese

Béchamel, remainder of spinach and cheese. Repeat third layer of lasagne, ending with Sauce Béchamel on top. Sprinkle top with remaining grated Parmesan.

COOK'S TIP: Baking can be delayed at this point until just prior to serving time.

(3) Bake covered in aluminum foil for 50 minutes at 350 degrees or 1 hour and 15 minutes if lasagne has been refrigerated. Remove cover for last 10 minutes.

(4) *Service* Allow Lasagne to stand 10-15 minutes before slicing. Slice into 2-inch squares and serve right from baking dish. Place a sprig of crisp watercress beside each serving.

1 sprig watercress per serving

Braised Celery and Zucchini

(1) Wash 4 small zucchini with a soft brush. Split in half, then into thirds, making 6 long strips. Cut each strip into 1-inch lengths. Trim and peel 3 ribs celery and cut into similar lengths.

(2) Sauté 1 slivered onion and 1 pressed clove garlic in 2 tablespoons olive oil. Add zucchini and celery, ¼ cup water and 1 teaspoon instant chicken bouillon granules. Add ½ teaspoon salt and a little freshly ground black pepper. Cook, covered, shaking pan and turning once or twice until vegetables are cooked through but not mushy (about 8 minutes).

4 small zucchini
3 ribs celery
1 onion, slivered
1 clove garlic, pressed
2 tablespoons olive oil
¼ cup water
1 teaspoon instant chicken bouillon granules

½ teaspoon salt
Freshly ground black pepper

Toasted Garlic Bread

(1) Cream together ¼ pound softened butter and 1 small pressed clove garlic.
(2) Slice one loaf French bread on the oblique, and spread each slice with garlic butter.
(3) Place buttered bread on baking sheet and toast in a 375-degree oven for 15 to 18 minutes, turning once. Serve from basket lined with napkin.

¼ pound (½ cup) softened butter
1 small clove garlic, pressed
1 loaf French bread, sliced

Macedonia De Frutta Al Marsala
(Mixed Fruit in Marsala Wine)

Two to three hours before serving, thaw and open 3 packages quick-thaw frozen mixed fruit and place in glass bowl. Add ½ cup Marsala wine. Gently stir occasionally. Bring bowl to table and spoon servings into stemmed dessert dishes. Serve with "Pirouettes" if desired.

3 packages (13½-ounce) quick-thaw frozen mixed fruit
½ cup Marsala wine
1 box "Pirouettes" (rolled dessert cookies)

Artichokes with Tarragon Mayonnaise
Florentine Meat Balls
Risi Bisi   Tomatoes Niçoises
Marsala Pudding with Meringue

Valpolicella

For centuries, Florentines have been associated with fine food. The much documented Florentine family of De Medici, whose interests included banking and the arts, was also instrumental in developing the world's spice trade. They employed the finest chefs of the day and were known to pamper their palates. Consequently, when any dish, even the lowly meat ball, is preceded by the name Florentine, one begins to have great expectations for the quality of the dish.

Expectations will not go unrewarded with this version of Florentine meat balls. They are baked or simmered in a beautifully seasoned cooking base known as *mirepoix*. Mirepoix is made from equal parts of celery, onion, and carrots, which are uniformly and finely diced. It is used by chefs to enhance the flavor of food in a natural way. In this recipe, after the meat balls are browned, they are combined with a mirepoix base. As they simmer together, each imparts flavor to the other and a fine sauce develops naturally.

It goes without saying that an entrée which is cooked with such care deserves nothing but the best entourage. This fine dinner begins with whole, cold artichokes. The details of how to prepare, cook, and serve them as a first course are outlined here. You will make your own tarragon mayonnaise to use as a filling and sauce.

Risi Bisi is truly an elegant rice presentation which has its origin in and around Venice. The rice derives its distinguished flavor from being cooked in white wine and chicken broth. This version contains a tiny bit of prosciutto and little green peas. At the end of cooking, it is embellished with a handful of grated Parmesan cheese. You will find this dish most enjoyable with Florentine meat balls. It can also provide a change-of-pace dish to serve with grilled chops or steaks.

For added color on the plate, and for a flavor born in heaven, try Tomatoes Nicoises. These baked tomatoes are filled with garlic and herb-seasoned breadcrumbs bound together with olive oil. Again, this is a dish to be enjoyed with a variety of menus. These tomatoes make a particularly good accompaniment for charcoal grilled meats.

A cool and satisfying dessert for this menu is found in a simple pudding topped with meringue. It contains many of the textures and flavors found in more elaborate Italian desserts, but is quick to make and can be served from an attractive baking dish.

Artichokes with Tarragon Mayonnaise

Advance Preparation (1) Remove any bruised or discolored leaves from 8 uniform artichokes. Cut the stem off evenly with bottom row of leaves. With a sharp knife remove the very top of the artichoke in a straight line. With kitchen shears remove the spiny tips of each leaf. Work quickly with each artichoke and drop into acidulated water (1 teaspoon vinegar or lemon juice per quart of water) as soon as each is trimmed.

8 artichokes
Acidulated water, while preparing

(2) Fill a large enameled pot with 8 to 10 quarts of water. Add 3 tablespoons each salt and lemon juice and bring to a rapid boil. Add the artichokes and simmer, uncovered, for about 20 minutes. Remove artichokes and turn upside down to cool and drain. When the artichokes are cool enough to handle, spread them open and remove the small yellow inner leaves and the choke. It should come out in one piece. The very bottom can then be scraped clean with a spoon.

8 to 10 quarts boiling water
3 tablespoons salt
3 tablespoons lemon juice

Final Preparation and Service Give each artichoke a little squeeze in a kitchen towel to remove as much moisture as possible. Fill centers with fresh homemade tarragon mayonnaise.

When dining, guests will pull off the leaves one at a time and dip them in mayonnaise. The leaves are pulled through the teeth to yield the edible portion, and the tough fibrous portion is discarded. When all the leaves have been enjoyed, the *bottom* comes into view. It is scraped clean of any remaining choke and cut into bite-size pieces with a knife and fork.

Tarragon Mayonnaise

Place 2 tablespoons white wine vinegar and 1 teaspoon each salt and dry mustard in top of blender. Add ½ teaspoon tarragon and 1 sprig minced parsley. Add 1 whole egg and ¼ cup salad oil. Blend a few seconds and add ¾ cup additional salad oil in a slow, steady stream. Cease blending when mixture becomes thick and smooth.

2 tablespoons white wine vinegar
1 teaspoon salt
1 teaspoon dry mustard
½ teaspoon tarragon
1 sprig parsley, minced
1 whole egg
1 cup salad oil

Florentine Meat Balls (Meatballs in Savory Vegetable Sauce)

Advance Preparation (1) *Meat Balls* Combine 2 pounds ground chuck, 2 teaspoons salt, a little freshly ground black pepper, ½ cup finely minced parsley, ¼ cup grated Parmesan cheese, 1 pressed clove garlic and 1 teaspoon each oregano, basil, and thyme. Soak 2 slices white bread in milk to saturate, and beat into meat mixture.

Beat 2 eggs until frothy and add to meat mixture. Shape mixture into 1-inch balls and roll in flour. Set aside until flour no longer appears white.

(2) Heat 2 tablespoons each olive oil

2 pounds ground chuck
2 teaspoons salt
Freshly ground black pepper
½ cup finely minced parsley
¼ cup grated Parmesan cheese
1 clove garlic, pressed
1 teaspoon oregano
1 teaspoon basil
1 teaspoon thyme
2 slices white bread, soaked in milk to saturate
2 eggs, beaten
Flour

2 tablespoons olive oil

and butter in skillet and brown the meat balls. Remove meat balls to an ovenproof serving dish.

(3) *Seasoned Cooking Base* Pour off all but 2 tablespoons grease from skillet. Sauté 1 cup each finely diced carrot, onion and celery until limp. Stir in 2 tablespoons flour and 1 can condensed beef broth. Stir until smooth and of sauce consistency. Pour over meat balls. Cover and reserve.

COOK'S TIP: Cooking may be delayed at this point until 1 hour before serving time.

(4) *Final Preparation* Place meat balls in a 375-degree oven. Bake, covered, 1 hour. Remove from oven and sprinkle with 1 to 2 tablespoons lemon juice, and 1 tablespoon finely minced parsley.

2 tablespoons butter

1 cup finely diced carrot
1 cup finely diced onion
1 cup finely diced celery
2 tablespoons flour
1 can (10½-ounce) condensed beef broth

2 tablespoons lemon juice
1 tablespoon finely minced parsley

Risi Bisi (Rice cooked in Wine with Green Peas and Cheese)

(1) Sauté 1 finely diced onion and 2 tablespoons minced prosciutto in 2 tablespoons each butter and olive oil. (If prosciutto is unavailable, proceed without it.) Add 1½ cups converted rice and stir until rice is coated with oil.

(2) Add ½ cup dry white wine and simmer until liquid is absorbed. Add 2½ cups of the chicken broth and 1 package tiny frozen peas. Cover and cook until all liquid is absorbed, about 10 minutes.

1 finely diced onion
2 tablespoons minced prosciutto
2 tablespoons butter
2 tablespoons olive oil
1½ cups converted rice

½ cup dry white wine
3½ cups condensed chicken broth (canned or made double-strength from cubes)
1 package (10-ounce) tiny frozen peas

(3) Add 1 additional cup of chicken broth and cook another 10 minutes. Remove from heat and stir in 2 tablespoons butter and ½ cup grated Romano or Parmesan cheese.

2 tablespoons butter
½ cup grated Romano or Paresan cheese

Tomatoes Niçoises (Baked Tomatoes in the Style of Nice)

Advance Preparation (1) Remove top ¼ from 8 medium, uniform tomatoes. Carefully remove seeds, leaving sectional walls intact. Sprinkle with salt and turn upside down to drain.
(2) *Filling* Combine 1½ cups fine bread crumbs, 1 clove pressed garlic, ½ cup finely minced parsley, a little freshly ground black pepper, and 1 teaspoon each basil, oregano and salt. Moisten crumb mixture with ½ cup olive oil. Spoon into tomato cases, packing rather firmly. Reserve until baking time.
Final Preparation Place tomatoes on baking sheet and bake in a 375-degree oven for 20 minutes. Serve as soon as possible.

8 medium, uniform tomatoes
Salt

1½ cups fine bread crumbs
1 clove garlic, pressed
½ cup finely minced parsley
Freshly ground black pepper
1 teaspoon basil
1 teaspoon oregano
1 teaspoon salt
½ cup olive oil

Marsala Pudding with Meringue

(1) *Ladyfinger Base* Butter an attractive serving dish, such as a ceramic quiche dish or a 9-inch au gratin dish. Line bottom and sides with ladyfingers, cutting them to fit the dish. Sprinkle with ¼ cup Marsala wine and set aside.
(2) *Pudding* Combine ½ cup sugar,

1 dozen ladyfingers
¼ cup Marsala wine

½ cup sugar

2 tablespoons cornstarch and a dash salt in heavy saucepan. Stir in 1¾ cups milk and whisk steadily over moderate heat until mixture comes to a full boil. Whisk in 3 well-beaten egg yolks. Continue cooking 1 minute. Pour mixture over ladyfingers.

(3) *Meringue* In large mixer bowl, combine the three egg whites, ¼ teaspoon cream of tartar and a dash salt. Beat until soft peaks have formed. Add 3 tablespoons granulated sugar, one spoonful at a time. Beat until stiff, glossy peaks have formed. Spread over pudding. Bake at 350 degrees for 10 to 12 minutes or until lightly browned. Cool. Serve at room temperature.

(4) *Service* Bring dish to table and serve with a spoon.

2 tablespoons cornstarch
Dash salt
1¾ cups milk
3 eggs, separated

3 egg whites (above)
¼ teaspoon cream of tartar
Dash salt
3 tablespoons granulated sugar

Antipasto Piatto Grande
Veal Parmigiana   Buttered Mushroom-Spaghetti
Insalata Verde
Zabaglione

Brolio Chianti Classico

The final menu in this series begins with an attractive antipasto platter which can be assembled in the afternoon before your party. Tiny tomatoes filled with tuna, cubes of melon wrapped in prosciutto, ripe olives, pepperoncini and assorted things "Italiano" are artfully arranged on a base of thinly sliced Genoa salami. This course, when served from a side table in the living room, adds much to the festive mood of the occasion.

Spaghetti and meat balls, so many years America's favorite party food, have settled comfortably into acceptance at routine family dinners. They might well be replaced as an entrée for party menus by Veal Parmigiana. Many ways more suitable for entertaining, Veal Parmigiana can be prepared up to the point of baking in the afternoon. It is placed in the oven just before needed. It comes out of the oven bubbling deliciously in a topping of cheese and yummy tomato sauce. Freshly cooked buttered spaghetti, tossed with sautéed mushrooms, is our choice to accompany this savory entrée.

This dinner should be enjoyed with a good red wine, possibly an Italian Chianti. Many Italian winegrowers now ship under the organizational name Chianti Classico. These wines may be recognized by a small black seal with a red rooster in the center, found on the neck of the bottle. Look for this seal the next time you are shopping. You will see it on Brolio wines as well as on others.

Many good cooks are afraid to try making the delicious wine custard known as Zabaglione. Actually, it is not difficult to make. If you simply follow the instructions given in this recipe, you will find that it makes itself. Men love to make Zabaglione, and it is a good task to turn over to your husband. He will no doubt attract an audience.

This version of Zabaglione is lighter than most, as beaten egg whites are folded into the yolk mixture at the end. It is lovely to serve in wine glasses and goes well with a delicate dessert cookie.

Antipasto Piatto Grande (Large Platter of Assorted Appetizers)

(1) *Salami* Line a large (12" x 18") platter with overlapping slices of Genoa-style salami, completely covering platter. Place an unopened 2-ounce jar of Italian Antipasto in center of platter, as a decoration.

1 pound Genoa salami, thinly sliced
1 jar (2-ounce) Italian Antipasto

(2) *Eggs* Hard cook 6 eggs and split in half lengthwise. Spread each egg completely with mayonnaise and

6 hard-cooked eggs
½ cup mayonnaise

place ½ a rolled anchovy on top of each. Arrange spoke-fashion around jar of Antipasto.

(3) *Cherry Tomatoes Filled with Tuna* Remove top ¼ of 18 cherry tomatoes, and carefully scoop out insides. Combine ½ cup well-drained tuna, 2 tablespoons mayonnaise, 1 teaspoon minced green onion and ½ teaspoon Beau Monde. Use to fill tomatoes. Place a tiny flowerette of parsley on top of each tomato. Arrange at random on platter.

(4) *Melon and Prosciutto* Cut ½ a honeydew melon or cantaloupe into 1-inch cubes. Split ¼ pound thinly sliced prosciutto lengthwise into strips and wrap around cubes of melon. Secure with toothpicks. Scatter at random on platter.

(5) *Pepperoncini and Ripe Olives* Fill remaining spaces on platter with drained pepperoncini. Roll ripe olives in small amount of olive oil and add to platter in random fashion.

(6) *Watercress* Use several crisp sprigs watercress to tuck in at random as a final garnish.

(7) *Service* Provide hors-d'oeuvres plates and serve with freshly sliced Italian bread and butter, or bread sticks.

1 can (2-ounce) rolled anchovies

18 cherry tomatoes
½ cup tuna
2 tablespoons mayonnaise
1 teaspoon green onion, minced
½ teaspoon Beau Monde
18 tiny flowerettes of parsley

½ honeydew or cantaloupe
¼ pound prosciutto, thinly sliced
Toothpicks

12 pepperoncini (pickled Italian peppers), well drained
12 to 18 ripe olives, oiled

Several sprigs watercress

Freshly sliced Italian bread, with butter

Veal Parmigiana

Advance Preparation (1) *Veal* Have 1½ to 2 pounds leg of veal cut into ½-inch slices. To make scallops, di-

1½ to 2 pounds leg of veal sliced
1 cup flour

vide each slice into 3 or 4 pieces. Place each piece between sheets of waxed paper and pound to a thickness of ¼ inch. Dip in seasoned flour (1 cup flour, 1 teaspoon salt, ¼ teaspoon white pepper and ¼ teaspoon paprika) and shake off excess. Allow to stand while preparing tomato sauce.

(2) *Tomato Sauce* Sauté 1 large chopped onion, 3 cloves pressed garlic and 2 tablespoons minced parsley in 2 tablespoons olive oil. Add two 1-pound cans Italian tomatoes and break up with a fork. Add one 15-ounce can tomato sauce, and 1 cup water. Add 2 tablespoons sugar, ½ teaspoon cracked bay leaf and 1 teaspoon each basil, thyme and oregano. Add a little freshly ground black pepper and 1 teaspoon salt. Simmer 30 minutes.

(3) *Cheeses* Slice one 12-ounce package mozzarella cheese as thinly as possible. Grate and have ready 1 cup Romano or Parmesan cheese, not packed.

(4) Beat together 2 eggs and ¼ cup dry white Vermouth. Dip veal scallops first into egg mixture, then into fine bread crumbs. Add 2 tablespoons olive oil to skillet, heat and fry veal scallops about 3 minutes on each side or until lightly browned. Remove and drain on paper towels. Add olive oil as necessary and continue frying until all scallops have been browned.

(5) *Assembly* Lightly oil a flat bak-

1 teaspoon salt
¼ teaspoon white pepper
¼ teaspoon paprika

1 large onion, chopped
3 cloves, garlic, pressed
2 tablespoons minced parsley
2 tablespoons olive oil
2 cans (1-pound) Italian tomatoes
1 can (15-ounce) tomato sauce
1 cup water
2 tablespoons sugar
½ teaspoon cracked bay leaf
1 teaspoon basil
1 teaspoon thyme
1 teaspoon oregano
Freshly ground black pepper
1 teaspoon salt

1 package (12-ounce) mozzarella cheese
1 cup grated Romano or Parmesan cheese

2 eggs
¼ cup dry white Vermouth
2 cups fine bread crumbs
About ½ cup olive oil

ing dish. Spread a thin coating of tomato sauce on bottom. Place a layer of veal scallops on sauce and add about one-half the cheese. Mask completely with tomato sauce. Repeat, ending with cheese on top. Cover dish with lid or aluminum foil.

Cook's Tip: Dish may be set aside at this point and baked just prior to serving.
Final Preparation If dish is baked immediately, bake at 350 degrees for 1 hour. If dish is held and ingredients have become cold, bake at 350 degrees for 1½ hours. Remove cover during last 10 minutes so that cheese browns lightly.

Buttered Mushroom-Spaghetti

(1) Fill a 10 to 12-quart pot with water and add salt in the proportion of 1 teaspoon per quart. Add 1 tablespoon oil. Bring to rolling boil and add 1 pound spaghetti* a little at a time, making sure water does not cease to boil. Cook 8 to 10 minutes, uncovered.

10 to 12-quart pot of boiling salted water
1 tablespoon oil
1 pound spaghetti

(2) Meanwhile, wash and trim ½ pound fresh mushrooms. Slice from stem through cap and sauté until lightly browned in 2 tablespoons butter.

½ pound mushrooms, sliced and sautéed
2 tablespoons butter

(3) Warm a large ironstone bowl and place ¼ pound (½ cup) butter in bottom. Add ¼ cup finely minced parsley and the sautéed mushrooms.

¼ pound (½ cup) butter
¼ cup minced parsley

(4) When spaghetti is tender, but remains a little resistant to the bite,

drain off hot water and shake dry. Add to bowl and toss with mushroom mixture. Sprinkle with a little freshly ground black pepper. Taste and add salt as necessary.

*Cook's Tip: Using this same recipe, substitute broad egg noodles for spaghetti and add 1 cup shredded Swiss or Fontina cheese for a very good Mushroom Fettuccine.

Freshly ground black pepper
Salt to taste

Insalata Verde (Italian-Style Green Salad)

(1) *Greens* Remove bruised and unsound outer leaves from one head each Boston, Bibb, and leaf lettuce. Wash in cold water, swing in salad basket to remove excess water, and roll into large kitchen towels. Refrigerate until needed.

1 head Boston lettuce
1 head Bibb lettuce
1 head leaf lettuce

(2) *Italian Vinaigrette* Place 2 tablespoons each lemon juice and white wine vinegar in screw-top jar. Add 1 teaspoon salt, a little freshly ground black pepper, 1 small clove pressed garlic, ½ teaspoon oregano and 1 tablespoon each minced capers and parsley. When salt has dissolved add ½ cup olive oil and ¼ cup salad oil. Shake well.

2 tablespoons lemon juice
2 tablespoons white wine vinegar
1 teaspoon salt
Freshly ground black pepper
1 small clove garlic, pressed
½ teaspoon oregano
1 tablespoon minced capers
1 tablespoon minced parsley
½ cup olive oil
¼ cup salad oil
Salt and pepper to taste

(3) *Assembly* At serving time, break greens into chilled salad bowl. Discard hard cores. Toss with just enough Vinaigrette to make greens glisten. Taste and add salt and freshly ground black pepper as desired. Serve on

chilled salad plates after dinner plates have been removed.

Zabaglione (Marsala Wine Custard)

(1) Separate 6 eggs. Reserve 2 whites for another use. Place 4 whites in large mixer bowl. Add ¼ teaspoon cream of tartar and beat until frothy. Gradually add 4 tablespoons sugar while beating to the consistency of meringue. Reserve.

(2) Place the 6 yolks, ½ cup Marsala wine and 4 tablespoons sugar in a copper beating bowl, or in the top of a double boiler. Place over barely simmering water and beat with a wire whisk (or hand-held electric mixer) until yolks are light, fluffy, and quadrupled in volume. (About 8 minutes.) Remove from heat and fold in the beaten whites. Spoon into stemmed dessert dishes or wine glasses and serve at once, with ladyfingers or rolled dessert cookies on the side.

6 eggs, separated
¼ teaspoon cream of tartar
4 tablespoons sugar
½ cup Marsala wine
4 tablespoons sugar
Ladyfingers or dessert cookies, as desired

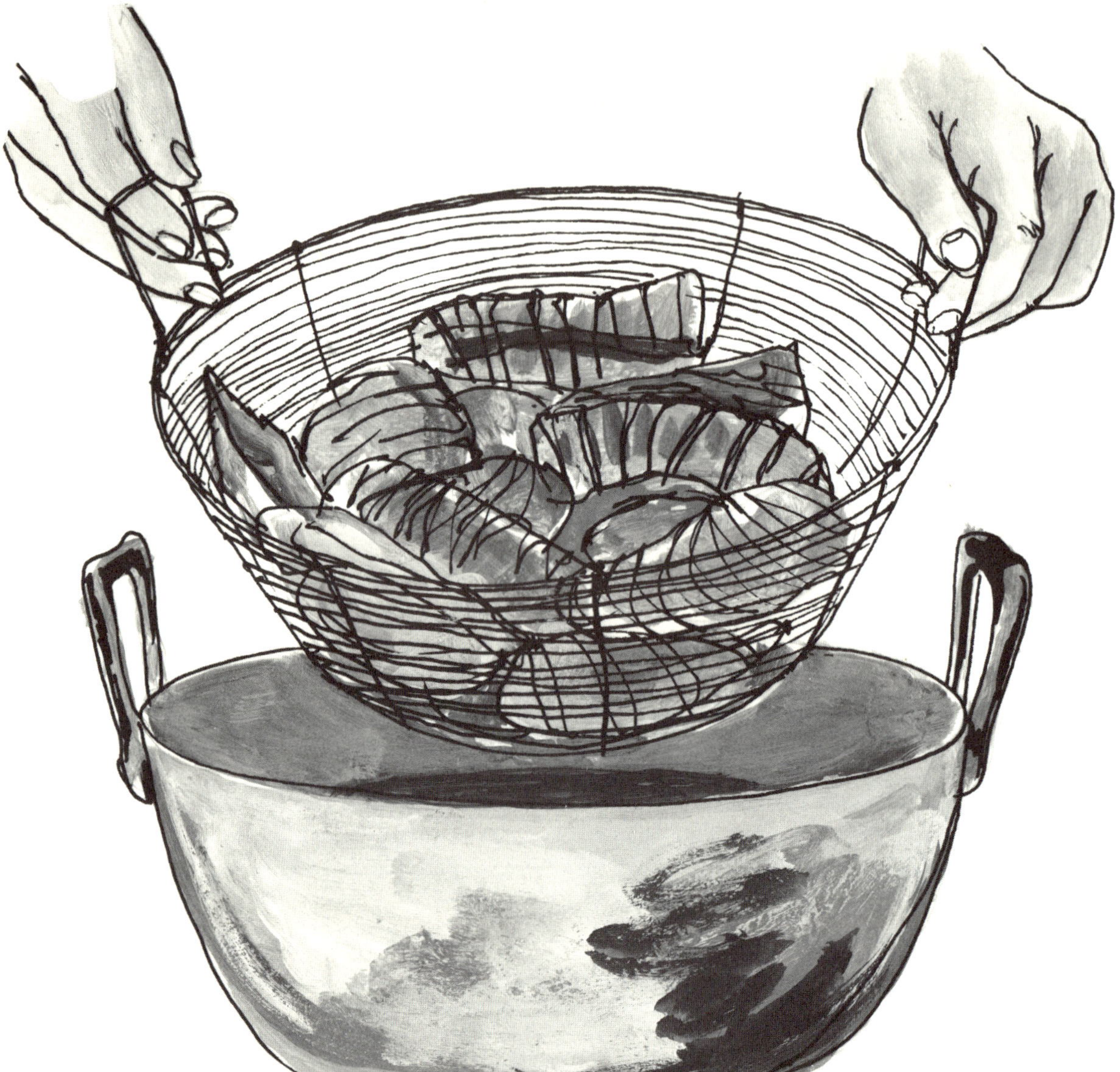

VIII BISTRO SUPPERS BY CANDLELIGHT

Red and white checked tablecloths, and elbows on the table: an intimate, relaxed atmosphere in which to enjoy these regional specialties originating in the provences of France.

Hors-D'Oeuvres Variés à la Niçoise
Bouillabaisse
Homemade French Bread
Riz Meringue

———

Rosé from Provence or Corsica, or Macon Blanc

"*A la Niçoise.*" What does it mean? Literally, "in the style of Nice," a resort town on the French Riviera. A little broader interpretation might be "in the style of Provence," the surrounding countryside. Geographically, it is the southern tip of France which borders on Italy and the Mediterranean. Gastronomically, it is the cookery of these areas. It is aromatic and spicy, and features garlic, thyme, fennel, rosemary, and bay leaf. It is olive oil and tomatoes. It is "creatures of the sea" and lamb. It is figs and melons; bouillabaisse and Salade Niçoise.

The first course of this menu is an hors-d'oeuvre presentation of the ingredients usually found in Salade Niçoise. These flavors are most appropriate to precede bouillabaisse and substantial enough for an otherwise light menu. Each item is properly seasoned and garnished, and served from an individual dish.

Many people think that an acceptable bouillabaisse cannot be made without the fishes of the Mediterranean, but it can. If you take special care in brewing an aromatic broth in which to poach a selection of domestic fish and shellfish, each according to its required cooking time, you can make not only an acceptable bouillabaisse, but a great one. The bouillabaisse in this menu is so well seasoned that you will not need the side dish "rouille" (garlic, saffron and hot pepper sauce) usually found on Provençal tables. It should be served with either a good bakery French bread or your own, which can be made from the recipe included here.

In Marseilles, local wines such as the rosés of Provence or the island of Corsica, are served with bouillabaisse. A dry white wine, such as Macon Blanc, would be equally enjoyable.

As a finale, you will enjoy this French version of rice pudding. It is substantial enough to placate the man in your life who might contend that "soup" is too light to be served as an entrée. This pudding is made by a classic method which gets the most out of the rice, both in texture and in consistency. It has a thin layer of apricot jam between the pudding and its baked-on meringue topping.

Hors-D'Oeuvres Variés à la Niçoise (Appetizer Presentation in the Style of Nice)

(1) *Green Beans Vinaigrette* Place ¼ cup water in a large skillet and add 2 packages partially thawed whole green beans. Cook, uncovered, 4 to 5 minutes or until crisp-tender. Immediately, toss with ¼ cup Sauce Vinai-

¼ cup water
2 packages (9-ounce) frozen whole green beans
¼ cup Sauce Vinaigrette (Page 24)
Salt to taste

grette and sprinkle with salt to taste. Refrigerate until needed. At serving time, drain the green beans and line them up in ravier (see page 47). Garnish top with Mimosa Garnish (Page 45) and 1 tablespoon chopped pimento.

(2) *French Potato Salad* Drain 2 cans sliced potatoes and rinse under cool running water. Dissolve 1 teaspoon instant chicken bouillon in 1/3 cup water in a large skillet. Add the potatoes and cook over high heat, shaking pan until all bouillon is absorbed. While potatoes are still hot, toss with ¼ cup Sauce Vinaigrette and 2 tablespoons each finely minced parsley and green onion. Place in ravier.

(3) *Ripe Olives* Open and drain one can ripe olives. Toss with 1 teaspoon olive oil. (Olive oil keeps the skins shiny and fresh-looking upon standing.)

(4) *Hard-Cooked Eggs* Hard cook 4 eggs and cut into quarters. Arrange in ravier.

(5) *Tomato Salad* Peel and slice 3 or 4 tomatoes. Arrange in ravier. Sprinkle with salt and drizzle first with olive oil and then with fresh lemon juice. Garnish top with finely minced parsley and green onion.

(6) *Tuna Vinaigrette with Anchovies* Open and drain 2 cans albacore tuna and separate into chunks. Arrange in ravier and drizzle with Sauce Vinaigrette. Open and drain one can rolled anchovies. Cut each in half, crosswise,

1 recipe Mimosa Garnish (Page 45)
1 tablespoon chopped pimento

2 cans (1-pound) sliced potatoes
1 teaspoon instant chicken bouillon
1/3 cup water
¼ cup Sauce Vinaigrette (Page 24)
2 tablespoons finely minced parsley
2 tablespoons finely minced green onion

1 can (7½-ounce) ripe olives
1 teaspoon olive oil

4 hard-cooked eggs (How to cook, Page 25)

3 or 4 tomatoes
Salt to taste
Olive oil, as desired
Lemon juice, as desired
1 sprig minced parsley
1 minced green onion

2 cans (7-ounce) albacore tuna
1 can rolled anchovies
2 tablespoons Sauce Vinaigrette (Page 24)

making two thinner rolls. Arrange at random among chunks of tuna.

Service Place all items for hors d'oeuvre in raviers or serving dishes of uniform size and shape. Line them up on a tray for service in the living room. Provide individual plates and forks for guests. Serve with bread sticks or freshly sliced French bread and butter.

Bouillabaisse (Mediterranean Fish Soup)

(1) *Aromatic Broth* Place ½ cup olive oil in soup kettle. Chop and sauté 2 medium onions, 2 carrots, 1 rib celery and 3 pressed cloves garlic. Add one large can tomatoes, 4 cups clam juice and 4 cups water. Bring to rapid boil.

(2) *Seasonings* Add several sprigs parsley, 1 bay leaf, ½ teaspoon fennel seeds, ⅛ teaspoon powdered saffron, 1 teaspoon orange peel, ⅛ teaspoon cayenne pepper, 1 tablespoon salt and a little freshly ground black pepper. Continue simmering for 40 minutes. Strain broth, discarding seasoning material and return broth to kettle.

COOK'S TIP: If possible, place a wire basket just smaller than the cooking kettle in the broth before adding fish. At the end of cooking time, the basket can be lifted out of broth, making it easy to keep the fish in whole pieces.

½ cup olive oil
2 medium onions, chopped
2 carrots, chopped
1 rib celery, chopped
3 cloves garlic, pressed
1 can (1-pound 14-ounce) tomatoes
4 cups clam juice
4 cups water

2 to 3 sprigs parsley
1 bay leaf
½ teaspoon fennel seeds
1/8 teaspoon powdered saffron
1 teaspoon orange peel
1/8 teaspoon cayenne pepper
1 tablespoon salt
Freshly ground black pepper

(3) *The Fish* As broth simmers add 8 small lobster tails. Allowing the broth to return to a boil after each addition, add one pound haddock, one pound cod, one pound halibut or flounder, one pound peeled and deveined shrimp and one pound scallops or crab meat. When available, add 8 or more clams in the shell. Allow all to simmer together 8 to 10 minutes following last addition.

Final Preparation and Service Carefully remove all seafood from broth and arrange it attractively on a heated platter. Garnish the top with finely minced parsley. Taste the broth and correct seasoning, if necessary. Place broth in a soup tureen. Guests may choose servings of fish and ladle the broth over it. Provide large, flat soup plates if possible. Serve with plenty of good crusty French bread, or make your own.

8 small lobster tails
1 pound haddock
1 pound cod
1 pound halibut, or flounder
1 pound shrimp, peeled and deveined
1 pound scallops or crab meat
8 clams in the shell

2 tablespoons finely minced parsley

Homemade French Bread

(1) Dissolve 2 packages active dry yeast in ¼ cup warm water in large mixer bowl. Add 2 cups additional warm water, 2 teaspoons salt and 2 tablespoons sugar. Stir in 3 cups sifted all-purpose flour, 1 cup at a time, and beat 3 to 5 minutes in mixer. Add a fourth cup of flour and beat by hand until dough is smooth and elastic. Add a fifth cup of flour and beat in as well as possible. Dough will be stiff.

2 packages active dry yeast
¼ cup warm water
2 cups warm water
2 teaspoons salt
2 tablespoons sugar
6½ cups sifted all-purpose flour
1 teaspoon vegetable shortening

(2) Measure out 1½ cups additional sifted flour and generously flour board with part of it. Turn dough onto floured board, cover and let rest about 10 minutes. Knead in remaining flour. By the time all the flour is absorbed by kneading, the dough should be smooth and satiny. Shape into ball.

(3) Place dough in a lightly greased bowl and cover lightly with a damp kitchen towel. Allow to rise in a warm place until double in bulk, (About 1½ hours.) Punch down and transfer to a lightly floured board. Divide in two equal parts and shape each into a long slender loaf.

(4) Dust a baking sheet with corn meal and place loaves on it. Allow to rise in a warm place until nearly doubled in size. Brush tops with cold water. With a razor blade, make a row of diagonal cuts across each loaf. Place in a 400-degree oven. Place a pan of hot water in bottom of oven. Bake 35 minutes. Brush the top with lightly salted water and continue baking 10 minutes. Remove from oven and place on kitchen towels to cool.

1 tablespoon corn meal

Riz Meringue (French-Style Rice Pudding)

(1) Simmer 1 cup converted rice and 1¾ cups water, covered, for 25 minutes or until all water is absorbed. Add 2 cups milk and simmer 5 minutes.

1 cup converted rice
1¾ cups water
2 cups milk

(2) Beat together 2 eggs, 2 egg yolks (reserve whites for meringue), ¼ teaspoon salt, 1 teaspoon vanilla and ½ cup sugar. Remove rice from heat and stir in the egg mixture.

(3) Place pudding in a buttered 1½ quart soufflé dish. Place soufflé dish in a shallow pan partially filled with hot water. Bake at 350 degrees for 40 minutes.

(4) *Meringue* Meanwhile, add a dash salt and ¼ teaspoon cream of tartar to 2 egg whites and beat until soft peaks form. Beat in 3 tablespoons sugar, one spoonful at a time, until peaks are firm and glossy.

(5) Remove rice pudding from oven after 40 minutes and spread the top with ¾ cup apricot jam. Spread meringue over jam. Return to oven and continue baking 10 to 12 minutes or until lightly browned. Serve the pudding while still warm from the soufflé dish at the table.

2 eggs
2 egg yolks
¼ teaspoon salt
1 teaspoon vanilla
½ cup sugar
1 teaspoon butter (for dish)

2 egg whites
¼ teaspoon cream of tartar
3 tablespoons sugar

¾ cup apricot jam

Herbed Beef Broth and Assorted Canapes
Coq-au-Vin
Alsatian Green Beans
Salade de Saison
Crêpes Suzette

A Beaujolais, such as Saint-Amour or Juliénas

Herbed beef broth in cups, and a selection of small cocktail sandwiches, are served from trays in the living room for the first course of this supper. This method of service is easier on the hostess than serving and clearing a seated first course. At the same time, it contributes to the festive mood of the party and is a signal to guests that the cocktail hour is over.

Europeans complain that we have bred too much flavor out of our poultry. This version of Coq-au-Vin cleverly conceals that fact, if indeed it is a fact. Unless otherwise stated, Coq-au-Vin is made with a red wine, usually Burgundy. When cooking with wine, remember that the alcoholic content is exhausted during cooking, leaving behind only the residual flavor of the wine. Therefore, the wine used in cooking should be of drinking quality.

This Coq-au-Vin, rich in the residual flavors of red wine, will be much enjoyed when served with red wine. I have suggested a Beaujolais.

If desired, you may serve little boiled potatoes on the side, although a good French bread usually will suffice. Alsatian green beans contrast nicely with the richness of this dish.

A simple green salad could be served between the entrée and the dessert in this menu. One made with seasonal greens and tossed with a tangy vinaigrette would be perfect. The purpose of a salad at this point in the menu is to freshen the palate. Flavors that follow such a break come through with more clarity. In this menu, a salad course could also occupy your guests while you are getting organized for the grand finale, Crêpes Suzette.

You will find this presentation of Crêpes Suzette much less difficult than you'd think. Yet all the fun of a chafing dish presentation remains to enthrall host and guest alike.

Herbed Beef Broth

Place 3 cans beef broth in saucepan. Add 1½ soup cans water. Add 1 small chopped onion, 1 chopped carrot and 1 rib chopped celery. Add ½ teaspoon thyme, 1 bay leaf, 2 cloves and a sprig parsley. Simmer gently for 25 to 30 minutes. Strain and ladle into attractive mugs for living room service. Pass a tray of assorted canapés.

3 cans (10½-ounce) beef broth
1½ soup cans water
1 small onion, chopped
1 carrot, chopped
1 rib celery, chopped
½ teaspoon thyme
1 bay leaf
2 cloves
1 sprig parsley

Assorted Canapes

Deviled Ham on Rye Combine one can deviled ham, ¼ cup shredded raw carrot, 1 teaspoon finely minced green onion, ½ teaspoon Dijon mustard and 2 tablespoons mayonnaise. Spread slices of cocktail rye bread lightly with butter and fill each two slices with ham mixture. Makes 1 dozen. (Freeze and store surplus bread.)

1 can (4¾-ounce) deviled ham
½ cup shredded raw carrot
1 teaspoon minced green onion
½ teaspoon Dijon mustard
2 tablespoons mayonnaise
24 slices cocktail rye bread

Tiny Lobster Sandwiches Open and drain one can lobster. Mince the lobster meat and combine with 4 tablespoons mayonnaise, ¼ teaspoon tarragon and 1 teaspoon each minced green onion and parsley. Cut thinly sliced white bread into 1½-inch rounds. Spread rounds with butter and fill each 2 slices with lobster mixture. Spread outside edge of each sandwich with mayonnaise and roll in finely minced parsley. Makes 1 dozen.

1 can (5½-ounce) lobster
4 tablespoons mayonnaise
¼ teaspoon tarragon
1 teaspoon minced green onion
1 teaspoon minced parsley
1-pound loaf thin sliced sandwich bread
Softened butter, for spreading
Mayonnaise
2 tablespoons finely minced parsley

Watercress Roll-Ups Cream together ¼ pound butter, ½ teaspoon Beau Monde seasoning and enough finely minced watercress to generously fleck the butter with green. Select and reserve 12 well-formed sprigs of watercress. Trim 12 slices extra-thin sliced buttercrust bread into 3-inch squares. Spread each square with butter mixture and place sprigs of watercress in center. Roll up so that leaves extend beyond ends of rolls. Makes 1 dozen.

¼ pound butter
½ teaspoon Beau Monde seasoning
1 to 2 bunches watercress
12 slices extra-thin sliced buttercrust bread

Coq-Au-Vin (Chicken in Burgundy Wine Sauce)

Advance Preparation (1) Heat 2 tablespoons each butter and vegetable oil in Dutch oven. Brown 2 quartered frying chickens on all sides. You may have to do a few pieces at a time. As soon as all pieces are browned, pour off excess fat (reserving 4 tablespoons for sauce) and return all pieces to Dutch oven.

(2) Warm ¼ cup brandy, ignite and pour over chicken.

(3) *Sauce* Place 4 tablespoons cooking fat (reserved in Step 1) in another saucepan. Sauté one minced medium onion, 2 pressed cloves garlic and ½ cup finely cubed ham. Stir in 4 tablespoons flour, 1½ teaspoon salt, 1 teaspoon thyme and ½ teaspoon freshly ground black pepper. Continue cooking until flour has browned lightly. Whisk in 1½ cups each chicken bouillon and red Burgundy wine. Cook until smooth and pour over chicken in Dutch oven.

COOK'S TIP: At this point the Coq-au-Vin can be covered and refrigerated until baking time, or even overnight.

(4) If baked immediately, bake at 350 degrees 1½ hours. If it has been refrigerated, bake chicken at 350 degrees for 2 hours.

Final Preparation (1) About 30 minutes before serving time, braise 1 pound frozen small whole onions by

2 tablespoons butter
2 tablespoons oil
2 frying chickens, quartered

¼ cup brandy

4 tablespoons cooking fat reserved from Step 1
1 medium onion, minced
2 cloves garlic, pressed
½ cup finely cubed ham
4 tablespoons flour
1½ teaspoon salt
1 teaspoon thyme
½ teaspoon black pepper
1½ cups chicken bouillon
1½ cups red Burgundy wine

package directions. Wash 1 pound button mushrooms and trim away stems flush with bottom of caps. Sauté in 2 tablespoon butter until lightly browned. Reserve.

(2) At serving time transfer chicken to heated serving platter, leaving sauce in Dutch oven. Taste sauce and correct seasoning. If necessary to thicken, do so with 1 tablespoon cornstarch dissolved in 1 tablespoon cold water. Add prepared onions and mushrooms to sauce and spoon over chicken on platter. Garnish top with 2 tablespoons finely minced parsley.

COOK'S TIP: Both entrées and desserts employ the cooking method known as flambéing. To do this, spirits of 80 proof or more are warmed to release their vapors. The vapors form just above the surface of the liqueur or brandy and ignite automatically when they come in contact with an open flame. Remember, spirits must be *warmed* in order to ignite, but *overheating* can exhaust alcoholic content before vapors come in contact with flame. When this happens, some cooks are mystified that their spirits fail to ignite. There is less danger of this happening if spirits are warmed in a separate pan, then ignited, and poured over contents of dish, rather than heating spirits along with the food to be flambéed.

For all-purpose flambéing, acquire a bottle of Cognac or a good California brandy. Any of the fruit-fla-

1 pound frozen small whole onions
1 pound button mushrooms
2 tablespoons butter

1 tablespoon cornstarch, dissolved in 1 tablespoon water (if needed)
2 tablespoons finely minced parsley

vored brandies, bourbon or rum can be used for desserts.

Alsatian Green Beans (Green Beans in the Style of Alsace)
(1) Place ¼ cup water in large skillet. Add 2 packages partially thawed whole green beans and ½ teaspoon summer savory. Simmer, uncovered, turning once or twice, until all water is evaporated. Reserve.
(2) Sauté 4 slices bacon until crisp. Remove; crumble and reserve. Pour off all but 1 tablespoon bacon grease. Add 2 sliced shallots; sauté briefly.
(3) Combine ½ cup water and 1 teaspoon each instant chicken bouillon granules, cornstarch, salt and white wine vinegar. Add to shallots. Return green beans and bacon. Simmer until liquid thickens and beans are glazed. Remove to heated serving dish and sprinkle with 2 tablespoons finely minced parsley.

¼ cup water
2 packages (9-ounce) frozen whole green beans
½ teaspoon summer savory

4 slices bacon
1 tablespoon bacon grease
2 shallots, sliced

½ cup water
1 teaspoon instant chicken bouillon granules
1 teaspoon cornstarch
1 teaspoon salt
1 teaspoon white wine vinegar
2 tablespoons finely minced parsley

Salade de Saison (Seasonal Green Salad)
(1) Select 2 or more salad greens from *Checklist for Salad Greens* on Page 45. Wash and prepare them as outlined in accompanying recipe.
(2) At serving time, break green into chilled salad bowl. Toss with Sauce Vinaigrette à la Moutarde (Page 30). Garnish each serving with herb-seasoned salad croutons.

2 or more salad greens, prepared for salad (Page 29)
1 recipe Sauce Vinaigrette à la Moutarde (Page 30)
1 box (7-ounce) herb-seasoned salad croutons

Crêpes Suzette

Advance Preparation (1) *Crêpes for Dessert* Combine in top of blender 1 cup cold water, 1 cup milk, 4 eggs, ½ teaspoon salt, 2 cups sifted all-purpose flour, 4 tablespoons melted butter and 1 tablespoon each sugar and brandy. Blend well and refrigerate at least 2 hours. Strain batter before frying crêpes.
(2) Fry 2 to 3 crêpes per serving by directions on Page 50.
(3) *Orange Butter for Finishing* Cream together ½ pound softened butter and ½ cup granulated sugar. Add the grated rind from 2 oranges, 2/3 cup fresh orange juice, and 3 tablespoons Grand Marnier or Cointreau.

Final Preparation and Chafing Dish Service Assemble chafing dish with burner on a tray. Place prepared crêpes in an attractive container. Spoon orange butter into an interesting crock. Have at hand one bottle Grand Marnier or Cointreau, a fork and spoon for handling, a small flaming-pan, matches, and warm dessert plates.

Method Light burner and heat finishing pan of chafing dish. Add a spoonful of orange butter to pan and when it has melted and begun to foam, lay a crêpe in it. Handling the crêpe with a fork and spoon, rotate it to heat through, turn once, and finally fold it into quarters. Move it to the outside edge of pan. Repeat this process with

1 cup cold water
1 cup milk
4 eggs
½ teaspoon salt
2 cups all-purpose flour
4 tablespoons melted butter
1 tablespoon sugar
1 tablespoon brandy

½ pound butter
½ cup granulated sugar
Grated rind of 2 oranges
2/3 cup fresh orange juice
3 tablespoons Grand Marnier or Cointreau

INGREDIENTS AND EQUIPMENT CHECKLIST
Chafing dish
Crêpes (from Step 2)
Orange butter (from Step 3)
1 bottle Grand Marnier or Cointreau
Fork and spoon
Flaming-pan (4 to 6-inch copper skillet with long handle)
Matches
Dessert plates and forks

butter and crêpes until all butter is used up and you have finished the required number of crêpes. Pour ¼ cup Grand Marnier or Cointreau into small flaming-pan. Heat over flame of chafing dish and ignite.* Pour, while flaming, over crêpes. Tip the pan so that sauce accumulates on one side, and baste crêpes with sauce until flame dies. Serve at once.

Alternate Service Method Any time in the afternoon before your party, spread prepared crêpes generously with Orange Butter. Fold into quarters and arrange them in overlapping rows in an attractive oven-to-table baking dish. Cover and reserve. Fifteen minutes before serving time, sprinkle the crêpes generously with granulated sugar. Place them in a preheated 400-degree oven. Bake until bubbling and delicately browned. Bring the dish to the table and flambé the crêpes as for chafing dish presentation.

*See Cook's Tip Page 164.

Tomato-Corn Chowder
Choucroute Garnie
New Potatoes   Dijon Mustard
Light and Dark Soft Rolls
Black Cherry Cheesecake

Beer

When sauerkraut was introduced to the French, something great was bound to happen. And it did—Choucroute Garnie!

In Alsace, where France borders on Germany, sauerkraut is simmered for long periods of time in a mixture of white wine, herbs, juniper berries (you may substitute gin for juniper berries in most recipes) and aromatic vegetables. A variety of sausages and pork products can be cooked right along with the sauerkraut, or they can be cooked separately. At serving time, these hearty and flavorful foods are arranged attractively on a huge platter, the presentation of which dictates the mood of the evening. It will be festive.

A few years back when Americans began to struggle with ever-expanding waistlines, the innocent little potato, bearing more than its share of the blame, fell into disfavor. Now it is coming back, particularly on party menus which are inspired by continental cookery. In this menu, little boiled potatoes provide a mild counterpoint to the piquancy of the sauerkraut.

Tomato and Corn Chowder is a hearty first-course soup, and is perfect to precede this sauerkraut menu. My students tell me that this chowder quickly becomes a family favorite. They love serving it with sandwiches for hurry-up family suppers.

This menu, which spans the banks of the Rhine River to embrace the specialties of two cultures, finds a happy and appropriate ending in Black Cherry Cheesecake. It is as light and delicate as the French would like it to be, and as flavorful and colorful as the Germans would have it.

Tomato-Corn Chowder

(1) Sauté in 2 tablespoons butter, 2 minced green onions, ½ green bell pepper, minced, and 1 rib minced celery. When cooked through but not brown, add one large can tomatoes. Break up with fork and add two cans shoe peg whole kernel corn. Add 1 teaspoon salt and a little freshly ground black pepper. Cook 5 minutes.

2 tablespoons butter
2 green onions, minced
½ green bell pepper, minced
1 rib celery, minced
1 can (1-pound 14-ounce) tomatoes
2 cans (12-ounce) white shoe peg corn
1 teaspoon salt
Freshly ground black pepper

(2) Meanwhile, bring 1 quart milk to scalding point.

(3) Stir ½ teaspoon baking soda into tomato mixture and add the hot milk. Do not allow to boil after adding milk.

1 quart milk
½ teaspoon baking soda

Choucroute Garnie (French-Style Sauerkraut with Pork and Sausages)

Advance Preparation (1) *Sauerkraut* Open and drain three 1-pound cans Bavarian-style sauerkraut. Rinse under cold running water and squeeze dry. Place in casserole with ½ cup dry white wine, ¼ cup gin, 1 cup chicken bouillon and 2 tablespoons sugar.

(2) *Vegetable-Herb Bouquet* Tie together in cheesecloth, 1 carrot, 1 rib celery, 1 onion stuck with 2 cloves, 1 bay leaf, 1 sprig parsley and ½ teaspoon thyme. Imbed in sauerkraut. Bake casserole, covered, at 350 degrees for 2 hours.

(3) *Additions* During last half hour of baking, place 1-pound ham sausage on top of sauerkraut and continue baking. Meanwhile, sauté 1 pound sliced Canadian bacon, remove from pan and reserve. In same pan, fry 8 smoked pork chops until done. Simmer 1 to 2 pounds Polish sausage in boiling water for 20 to 25 minutes. Keep all meats and sausages warm. *Final Preparation* Remove seasoning bundle from sauerkraut. Transfer sauerkraut to heated serving platter. Cut sausages into serving pieces and ar-

3 cans (1-pound) Bavarian-style sauerkraut
½ cup dry white wine
¼ cup gin
1 cup chicken bouillon
2 tablespoons sugar

1 carrot
1 rib celery
1 onion stuck with 2 cloves
1 bay leaf
1 sprig parsley
½ teaspoon thyme
Cheesecloth

1 pound ham sausage
1 pound Canadian bacon, sliced
8 smoked pork chops
1 to 2 pounds Polish sausage

range with chops on top. Surround with boiled new potatoes and serve with Dijon mustard.

Boiled New Potatoes

Pare 1½ to 2 pounds new potatoes. Drop into boiling salted water (1 teaspoon salt per quart of water). Simmer, covered, 20 to 25 minutes or until tender. Drain and shake dry. Add 2 tablespoons melted butter. Roll potatoes to coat evenly.

1½ to 2 pounds new potatoes
Boiling salted water to cover
2 tablespoons butter

Black Cherry Cheesecake

(1) *Crust* Combine 1 cup zwieback crumbs, 2 tablespoons sugar, ½ teaspoon cinnamon and 3 tablespoons melted butter. Press into bottom of an 8-inch springform pan.

(2) *Cream Cheese Filling* Cream 3 packages softened cream cheese in large mixer bowl. Add ½ teaspoon salt and 3 tablespoons light rum. Separate 4 eggs and beat the yolks into cheese mixture. Add a pinch of salt and ¼ teaspoon cream of tartar to the 4 egg whites and beat until frothy. Gradually add 1 cup granulated sugar, beating until firm glossy peaks have formed. Fold whites into cheese mixture. Turn onto prepared crust in springform pan. Bake at 350 degrees for 35 to 40 minutes, or until set. Remove from oven and increase temperature to 450 degrees. Spread with Sour Cream Topping, return to

1 cup zwieback crumbs
2 tablespoons sugar
½ teaspoon cinnamon
3 tablespoons melted butter

3 packages (8-ounce) cream cheese, softened
½ teaspoon salt
3 tablespoons light rum
4 eggs, separated
Pinch of salt
¼ teaspoon cream of tartar
1 cup granulated sugar

oven and bake 5 more minutes. Remove from oven and cool completely.

(3) *Sour Cream Topping* Combine one 12-ounce carton dairy sour cream with 2 tablespoons sugar and use as directed in Step 2.

1 carton (12-ounce) dairy sour cream
2 tablespoons sugar

(4) *Black Cherry Topping* Thaw and drain one package quick-thaw frozen dessert cherries, reserving juice. Stir 1 teaspoon arrowroot into juice and cook about one minute or until clear. Stir in the cherries and add 1 tablespoon Kirsch. Cool and spread on top of cooled cheesecake. Refrigerate until needed.

1 package (10-ounce) quick-thaw frozen dessert cherries
1 teaspoon arrowroot
1 tablespoon Kirsch

Rillettes de Tours
Sliced French Bread   Butter and Cornichons
Boeuf Bourguignon
Buttered New Potatoes
Salad with Lemon-Curry Vinaigrette
Profiteroles au Chocolat

With the Rillettes, Sancerre or Saumur
With the Boeuf, a red Burgundy, such as Clos de Vougeot

When you have invited more people than you can seat comfortably, you will need a special kind of menu such as this.

These recipes are planned for eight people, but all of them are easy to expand and the foods lend themselves to buffet service. The cooking is the "do ahead" variety, yet nothing is sacrificed for those with discriminating palates. This menu could easily be expanded to serve twenty-four or more.

As a first course, the pâté-like specialty of the Loire, Rillettes (re-yet), can be made days ahead. It can be served from a crock with sliced French bread and little pickles, and it stands up boldly to cocktails. It is also delicious with a crisp white wine from the same area, such as Sancerre or

Saumur. This version of Rillettes is greatly diminished in calories, while maintaining all of the flavors characteristic of the original.

Boeuf Bourguignon is by far the most appreciated of imported French stews. The depth of flavor produced by using classic methods of French cooking and lots of wine make this a distinguished and popular entrée for buffets. It adapts well to self-service and requires no knife for eating. It is served with little boiled potatoes and a full-bodied red Burgundy.

When serving this menu to a seated party of eight, you will find it best to serve your salad following the entrée, as suggested by its placement in the menu. For a crowd, you might provide a salad station with fresh plates, where guests may return to help themselves. Or, switch to a large platter of cold vegetables vinaigrette. Such vegetables provide all of the refreshing qualities of a green salad, but can be served on the same plate as the hot foods. (A tossed green salad should never be served on the same plate with warm foods.)

Profiteroles (pro-fee-tráuls) au Chocolat are a well-kept secret as far as "do ahead" desserts are concerned. If you have never made cream puffs, do not fear. They rarely ever fail to puff. They can be baked the day before, filled with ice cream a few hours prior to the party, and kept in the freezer until needed.

A casual and relaxed atmosphere is the natural outcome of a relaxed and confident hostess. Menus such as this one, with a lot of "do ahead" cooking, help to bring this about. By getting as much done ahead as possible, you will have lots of free time to decorate for your party and few last-minute details to keep you from your guests.

Rillettes de Tours
(Savory Minced Pork Pâte)

Cut 1½ pounds lean pork shoulder into 1-inch cubes. Brown the meat in ½ cup rendered chicken fat.* Transfer to casserole and add 1 bay leaf,

1½ pounds pork shoulder, cubed
½ cup chicken fat, rendered*
1 bay leaf

1 teaspoon thyme, ¾ teaspoon salt and a little freshly ground black pepper. Pour in boiling water to cover by ½ inch. Cover casserole tightly and bake at 300 degrees for 3 hours. Cool mixture sufficiently to handle safely, remove bay leaf and run through blender to purée. Pack into crock and seal with a layer of rendered chicken fat.

*COOK'S TIP: Of course you may obtain chicken fat from your butcher. Or, to provide a steady source of chicken fat, collect the bits of fat clinging to the carcasses of fryers as you use them for other purposes. Place the fat in see-through containers in the freezer. If necessary, you may substitute butter in this recipe.

To Serve Rillettes Remove chicken fat or butter from top and place crock on a tray with a container of tiny dilled gherkins, sliced French bread and butter. Guests may help themselves.

1 teaspoon thyme
¾ teaspoon salt
Freshly ground black pepper
Boiling water to cover
Additional chicken fat

Boeuf Bourguignon
(Burgundy-Style Beef Stew)

Advance Preparation (1) Cut a 6-ounce piece of salt pork into ½-inch dice and simmer in water to cover for 10 minutes. Drain and blot dry. Place in kettle with 2 tablespoons vegetable oil and cook until crisp. Remove with slotted spoon and reserve.

COOK'S TIP: By using rendered pork

6 ounces salt pork
Water to cover

fat to brown meats in French stews, we achieve the characteristic depth of flavor expected. If desired, however, you may use vegetable oil entirely.

(2) Cut a 4 to 5-pound chuck roast into 2-inch cubes and brown the meat in rendered pork fat. Make sure pieces of meat do not touch while browning. Remove browned meat and reserve.

4 to 5-pound chuck roast
Rendered pork fat (Step 1)

(3) Pour off excess fat and add ½ cup each finely diced carrot, celery and onion. Sauté until cooked through and return browned cubes of meat to kettle. Sprinkle with 2 tablespoons flour, 1 teaspoon salt and a little freshly ground black pepper. Cook until flour is lightly browned.

½ cup finely diced carrot
½ cup finely diced celery
½ cup finely diced onion
2 tablespoons flour
1 teaspoon salt
Freshly ground black pepper, to taste

(4) *Wine and Seasonings* Dissolve 5 bouillon cubes in 2½ cups water and combine with 2½ cups red wine. Add 2 tablespoons tomato paste, 1 teaspoon each thyme and crumbled bay leaf, a sprig of minced parsley and 2 pressed cloves garlic. Bring to boil and pour over meat. Stir in reserved cubes of salt pork. Cover container and place in a 350-degree oven. Bake about 3 hours or until meat is fork tender.

5 bouillon cubes
2½ cups water
2½ cups red wine
2 tablespoons tomato paste
1 teaspoon thyme
1 teaspoon crumbled bay leaf
1 sprig parsley, minced
2 cloves garlic, pressed
Reserved cubes of salt pork

Final Preparation A half hour before serving, sauté 1 pound mushroom caps and braise 1 pound frozen small whole onions by package directions. Add to beef. Correct seasoning at this time. If necessary, thicken stew with 1 tablespoon cornstarch dissolved in 1 tablespoon cold water. Sprinkle the

1 pound mushroom caps
1 pound frozen small whole onions
1 tablespoon cornstarch dissolved in 1 tablespoon water (if needed)
2 tablespoons finely minced parsley

top with finely minced parsley. Serve with boiled new potatoes.

Buttered New Potatoes
Prepare 1½ to 2 pounds new potatoes by recipe on Page 171.

One recipe potatoes (Page 171)

Salad with Lemon-Curry Vinaigrette
(1) Wash and prepare an assortment of the most tender salad greens, by directions on Page 29.
(2) *Lemon-Curry Vinaigrette* Rub chilled salad bowl with a cut clove of garlic. Place an egg yolk in bowl. Add 1 tablespoon lemon juice, 2 tablespoons white wine vinegar, 1 teaspoon salt and ½ teaspoon curry powder. Add ½ cup French olive oil by droplets while beating continuously with a stainless wire whisk.
(3) *Assembly* Lay prepared greens on top of dressing. Sprinkle with 2 tablespoons each finely minced parsley and green onion. Add 1 can artichoke hearts, drained and quartered. Toss gently in a rolling motion. Taste, add salt and pepper if necessary.

1 head Boston lettuce
2 or 3 heads Bibb lettuce
1 bunch leaf lettuce
1 clove garlic
1 egg yolk
1 tablespoon lemon juice
2 tablespoons white wine vinegar
1 teaspoon salt
½ teaspoon curry powder
½ cup French olive oil

2 tablespoons minced parsley
2 tablespoons minced green onion
1 can (14-ounce) artichoke hearts

Profiteroles au Chocolat
(Cream Puffs with Chocolate Sauce)
Advance Preparation (1) *Cream Puff Shells* Place 1 cup water, ¼ pound butter and ¼ teaspoon salt in saucepan. Bring to boil. As soon as butter has melted, stir in 1 cup flour and

1 cup water
¼ pound butter (½ cup)
¼ teaspoon salt
1 cup flour

continue stirring vigorously with wooden spoon until mixture has pulled away from sides of pan and formed a ball. Transfer to large mixer bowl and add 4 eggs one at a time, beating well after each addition.

(2) Using a pastry bag or 2 teaspoons, make small 1-inch mounds of dough on ungreased baking sheet. Place in a 425-degree oven for 20 minutes. After 20 minutes remove puffs from oven and lower temperature to 350 degrees. Make a small hole in the side of each puff, along the natural break line. Return to oven for 10 minutes. Remove from oven and cool on rack.

(3) *Chocolate Sauce* Place 8 ounces semi-sweet chocolate bits in saucepan with ½ cup each water and sugar. Bring to simmer and cook 5 minutes. Remove from heat and stir in ¼ cup each butter and rum. Transfer to attractive serving pitcher with ladle and keep warm.

8 ounces semi-sweet chocolate bits
½ cup water
½ cup sugar
¼ cup butter
¼ cup rum

Final Preparation Cut puffs in half and remove soft uncooked membrane. Fill each with vanilla ice cream. Place filled puffs on a serving dish in a mound and drizzle with chocolate sauce. Pass additional chocolate sauce.

1 pint French vanilla ice cream

COOK'S TIP: Filled puffs may be kept in the freezer a few hours, if done ahead.

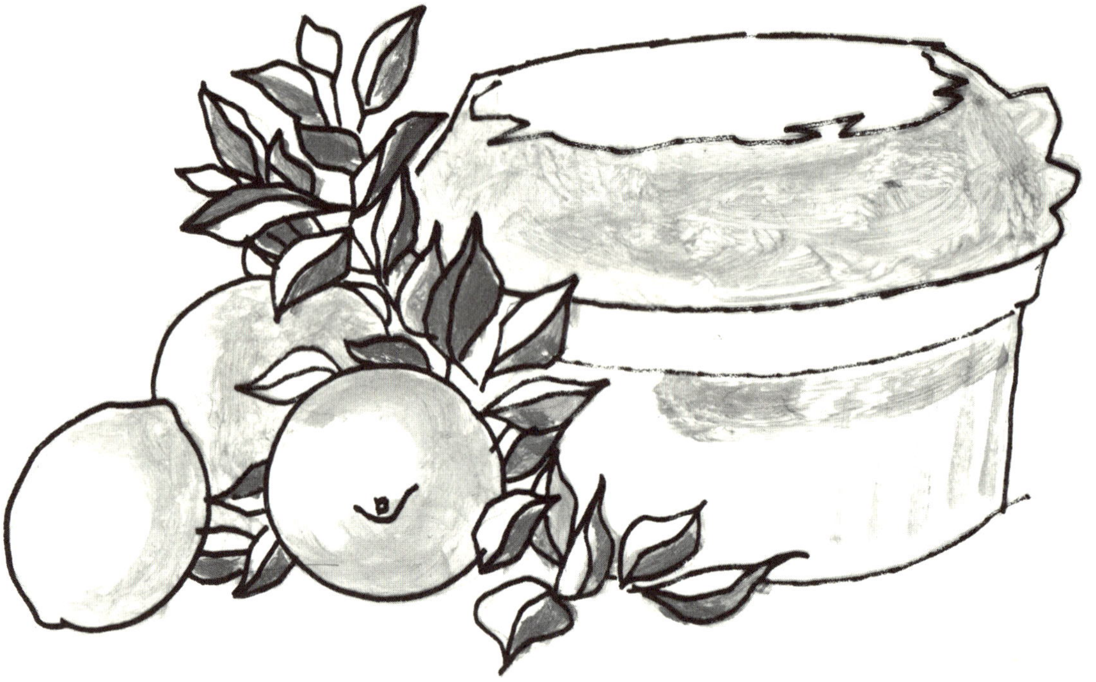

IX DINING OUT AT HOME: CONTINENTAL STYLE

Elegant continental-style dinners almost as easy on the hostess as dining out. Home provides the luxury of an unhurried atmosphere where fine food can be enjoyed with wine and where there is time to savor each beautiful course.

Terrine of Chicken Livers in Chopped Aspic
Homemade Melba Toast
Roast Loin of Pork and Red Cabbage
Duchess Potato Soufflé
Toasted Caraway Rye Bread
Swedish Apple Cake
———
Portuguese Rosé

When the wind is howling outside and you're in the mood to cook something really great, try this menu featuring Roast Loin of Pork and Red Cabbage.

As a first course you will be serving an excellent homemade chicken liver pâté. The pâté is accented with truffles and served from a terrine. Attractively topped with chopped aspic, this presentation is a good answer to the eternal question of how to make chicken livers *look* as good as they *taste*. This method of service does things for the pâté, is quick to do and is easy on the hostess.

The night before the party, a "dry marinade" of salt and herbs is rubbed into the surface of the pork. As it stands overnight, it thoroughly absorbs the flavors. The afternoon before your party, the roast can be browned on all sides and placed in its bed of beautifully seasoned red cabbage. At this point it can be held for roasting, or baked ahead and rewarmed. Actually, it loses nothing in being rewarmed, and possibly mellows a bit. For its final presentation, the roast is sliced and arranged on a platter. Completely surrounded by red cabbage, this dish needs no further garniture.

The mere suggestion of a last-minute soufflé may have many of you thumbing past this marvelous recipe for Duchess Potato Soufflé. But wait! This is a totally uncomplicated soufflé. Boiled potatoes, cream and eggs are all beaten together in the mixer. The combination is transferred to a buttered soufflé dish and *it* waits for *you*. This can be done anytime in the afternoon. Just before baking, the dish is topped with sour cream.

For dessert you will be serving a lovely apple cake from Sweden. Poached halves of apples are baked in a cake batter. Ground almonds replace flour in this dish, which more closely resembles a pudding than a cake. It can be baked and served in an attractive oven-to-table dish. At the table, each serving is topped with Cognac-flavored whipped cream.

Throughout this elegant repast your guests will have pondered the origins of these foods. Are they French, or are they Scandinavian? Actually, it is an eclectic menu and lends itself to a decorating motif reflecting either homeland. Zither music, Swedish polkas, and a wood-burning fire — what a lovely way to pass a long winter evening with good friends. However, be prepared to pity your lady guests. Their husbands will be grumbling all the way home, "Why don't you ever cook like that?"

Terrine of Chicken Livers in Chopped Aspic

Advance Preparation (1) *Chicken Liver Pâté* Sauté 1 small minced onion and 1 pressed clove garlic in ½ pound butter. Add 1 pound chicken livers, washed and trimmed, and continue cooking 10 minutes. Add 1 tablespoon Marsala or dry sherry, ½ teaspoon each salt, paprika, and allspice and a dash of Tabasco. Cool slightly.

1 small onion, minced
1 clove garlic, pressed
½ pound butter
1 pound chicken livers
1 tablespoon Marsala or dry sherry
½ teaspoon salt
½ teaspoon paprika
½ teaspoon allspice
Dash Tabasco

(2) Place ingredients in top of blender and add 2 tablespoon Cognac or bourbon. Blend until smooth. Finely mince the truffles* from a ⅞-ounce can and fold into pâté, including juice. Spoon mixture into a 2-cup terrine or soufflé dish, and refrigerate to cool completely.

2 tablespoons Cognac or bourbon
7/8-ounce can truffles*

*Cook's Tip: For the truffles you may substitute ¼ cup chopped pistachio nuts or toasted pecans if desired.

(3) *Aspic* Dissolve ½ envelope gelatin in ¾ cup canned beef consommé. Refrigerate until set.

½ envelope (1½ teaspoons) unflavored gelatin
¾ cup canned beef consommé

Final Preparation Remove aspic to chopping board and chop into small particles with a knife. Distribute evenly over top of pâté. Leave at room temperature for one hour prior to serving. Serve pâté from terrine with homemade Melba toast.

Homemade Melba Toast

Buy one pound extra-thin sliced buttercrust bread or, slice regular bread into ⅛-inch slices. Lay bread slices directly on racks of oven and toast at 225 degrees for 30 minutes or until lightly golden. Serve from napkin-lined silver tray.

1 pound extra-thin sliced buttercrust bread

Roast Loin of Pork and Red Cabbage

Advance Preparation (1) Have a loin of pork with a finished weight of 4 pounds, boned, rolled and tied. Combine 1 tablespoon salt and ½ teaspoon each thyme, black pepper, allspice and granulated garlic.* Rub into surface of pork. Rewrap in butcher paper and refrigerate a minimum of 2 hours, or overnight.

4-pound loin pork roast, boned, rolled and tied
1 tablespoon salt
½ teaspoon thyme
½ teaspoon black pepper
½ teaspoon allspice
½ teaspoon granulated garlic

*Cook's Tip: This salt and herb combination imparts the most fabulous flavor to cuts of pork that are dry roasted. Try it with country-style spareribs.

(2) When ready to cook, wipe away excess seasoning with a paper towel. Heat 2 tablespoons each butter and oil in a Dutch oven and brown the pork well on all sides. Remove and keep warm.

2 tablespoons butter
2 tablespoons oil

(3) Drain off excess fat and sauté 1 thinly sliced yellow onion and 2 thinly sliced carrots. Shred and add 1 medium head red cabbage and cook until limp. Chop two tart red apples

1 yellow onion
2 carrots
1 medium head red cabbage, shredded

and add to cabbage. Add 2 tablespoons red wine vinegar, ¼ cup brown sugar, 1 bay leaf and a grating of nutmeg. Stir in 1 cup dry white wine and simmer all ingredients 3 to 4 minutes. Push ingredients to one side and return the pork roast to Dutch oven. Spoon cabbage mixture over and around roast. Cover Dutch oven and bake in a 350-degree oven for 2 hours.

Final preparation Remove roast to heated serving platter and slice into serving pieces, keeping slices together in original shape of roast. Drain cabbage, discard bay leaf, and arrange around roast on platter. Dissolve 1 tablespoon cornstarch in 1 tablespoon cold water and stir into juices remaining in Dutch oven. Cook until clear and smooth. Spoon over the roast.

2 tart red cooking apples, chopped
2 tablespoons red wine vinegar
¼ cup brown sugar
1 bay leaf
Grating of nutmeg (1/8 teaspoon)
1 cup dry white wine

1 tablespoon cornstarch
1 tablespoon cold water

Duchess Potato Soufflé

Advance Preparation Pare and cut into large dice, 6 to 8 medium white potatoes. Drop into boiling salted water and cook, covered, about 25 minutes or until tender. Drain potatoes and shake dry over heat. Transfer to large mixer bowl and add 4 tablespoons butter, 1 teaspoon salt, ¼ teaspoon white pepper and a grating of nutmeg. Add ¾ cup light cream, 2 eggs and 2 egg yolks. Beat all together until light and fluffy. Butter a 2-quart soufflé dish and spoon in the potato mixture.

6 to 8 medium white potatoes
Boiling salted water to cover
4 tablespoons butter
1 teaspoon salt
¼ teaspoon white pepper
Grating of nutmeg (1/8 teaspoon)
¾ cup light cream
2 eggs
2 egg yolks

COOK'S TIP: At this point dish may be covered and held at room temperature until ready to bake.

Final Preparation Forty minutes prior to serving time, frost top of potatoes with 12 ounces (1½ cups) dairy sour cream. Sprinkle sour cream with Beau Monde seasoning and bake at 350 degrees for 30 to 35 minutes. Serve at once, while puffed.

1 carton (12-ounce) dairy sour cream (1½ cups)
Beau Monde seasoning

Toasted Caraway Rye Bread

Buy a 1-pound loaf of unsliced caraway rye bread. Trim away the crusts making loaf as square as possible. Split into 3 slices lengthwise, and then into fingers about ¾ inch square and 4 inches long. Brush all sides with melted butter and toast in a 350-degree oven for 20 to 25 minutes, turning once or twice.

1 (1-pound) loaf caraway rye bread, unsliced
¼ pound (½ cup) melted butter

Swedish Apple Cake

(1) *Apples* Select 4 tart cooking apples of uniform size. Pare and cut in half, removing cores.

4 tart cooking apples

(2) *Poaching Liquid* Combine 4 cups water, 1 cup sugar and the juice of one lemon and bring to boil. Drop the apple halves into poaching liquid and simmer 6 to 8 minutes. Remove apples, drain, and arrange rounded side up in a buttered flat baking dish.

4 cups water
1 cup sugar
Juice of one lemon

(3) *Cake Batter* In large mixer bowl cream together ½ cup butter and ¾ cup sugar. Add 3 eggs, one at a time,

½ cup butter
¾ cup sugar
3 eggs

beating well after each addition. Add ½ cup ground almonds (may be ground in blender) and the juice of half a lemon, (about 2 tablespoons). Spread mixture evenly over poached apples. Bake at 350 degrees for 25 minutes. Cool, but serve at room temperature with Cognac Chantilly.

½ cup almonds, ground
Juice of ½ lemon
1 recipe Cognac Chantilly (Page 9)

Caviar and Blini
Breasts of Chicken Sautés   Sauce au Vin Blanc
Soufflé aux Champignons
Broccoli Amandine
Strawberry Tart

Imported or Domestic Champagne, throughout

When the occasion dictates a little more formality than usual, you naturally expect a more complicated preparation schedule. This means more last-minute cooking and timing problems. At times such as these it is particularly important to be familiar with everything you are preparing, and to mentally designate which steps can be done before the guests arrive, and which must be done after they arrive. Employ the art of list making and write notes to yourself. These can be placed in a location for quick reference, such as on the refrigerator door.

Caviar and Blini, the most sophisticated of first courses, can be assembled in minutes. A surprising amount of preparation can be done in advance. The blini themselves can be baked the day before, wrapped in aluminum foil, and rewarmed just before needed. A bed of ice for the caviar can be prepared and kept in the freezer. Additions such as sieved egg, sour cream and minced onion can be prepared an hour or so ahead and held in the refrigerator. Then, with just a quick assembly job on a handsome tray, you can march triumphantly into the living room.

At the same time, your husband can uncork the first of

many bottles of Champagne to be served throughout this menu. If you have not already established a good working relationship with someone in the wine business, now is the time to start. He will help you choose Champagnes suitable for these foods, beginning with a very dry one (brut) and ending with a slightly sweeter one for the strawberry dessert.

Although last-minute cooking for this menu appears to be considerable, it can all be accomplished in forty-five minutes. When cooking requires the undivided attention of the hostess, guests are most appreciative and will understand your absence, knowing they will be beautifully rewarded with a fine dinner.

Now the plan: If the soufflé base is made ahead, you need only beat the whites and fold them into the base at the last minute. While the soufflé is baking you can sauté the breasts of chicken. This procedure is simplified if you use an electric skillet with exact temperature controls. The ingredients for the wine sauce can be standing by and quickly combined in the frypan after the chicken breasts are removed to a heated platter. Meanwhile, the broccoli can be simmering on the stove as you prepare the Amandine sauce which will be spooned on just before serving.

The strawberry tart can be fully assembled in the afternoon and kept refrigerated. This is a beautiful dessert and yet it is simplicity itself to prepare. All in all, this menu can start rumors about your ability as a cook and hostess . . . think about it when you make up your guest list.

Caviar and Blini
(Caviar with Russian Pancakes)

Advance Preparation (1) *Blini* Dissolve 1 envelope active dry yeast and 1 teaspoon sugar in ½ cup warm water in large mixer bowl. Add 1 cup milk at room temperature, 1½ cups sifted all-purpose flour, ½ teaspoon salt and 1/3 cup melted butter. Beat

1 envelope active dry yeast
1 teaspoon sugar
½ cup warm water
1 cup milk
1½ cups all-purpose flour
½ teaspoon salt
1/3 cup melted butter

until blended and add 3 eggs one at a time, beating well after each addition. Set aside in warm place for 1 hour.

(2) *To Fry* Heat a griddle or electric frypan and brush with melted butter. Spoon 2 tablespoons blini mixture onto griddle to make small pancakes about 2 inches across. Turn after 1 minute. As pancakes are lightly browned, place in stacks of 12 and wrap in aluminum foil. Place in warming oven until needed. Or, reheat at 350 degrees for 10 minutes.

Final Preparation (1) Fill a large bowl with crushed ice. Open a 4-ounce jar of imported or domestic caviar and place it in the center of ice (have a second jar in reserve). Place bowl on a tray and surround with smaller bowls of sour cream, minced green onion, sieved hard-cooked eggs, and wedges of lemon.

(2) *Service* As a seated first course, the host or hostess might wish to serve from a side table as follows: place about three blini on an hors-d'oeuvre plate. Spoon a little sour cream on each and place a small spoonful of caviar on each mound of sour cream. Sprinkle each serving with minced green onion and sieved hard-cooked egg. For living room service, allow guests to help themselves, but *do* provide plates.

3 eggs

Butter for frying
Aluminum foil

2 jars (4-ounce) caviar
1 carton (8-ounce) dairy sour cream
¼ cup finely minced green onion
2 hard-cooked eggs (Page 25)
Several wedges of lemon

Breasts of Chicken Sautes, Sauce au Vin Blanc (Sauteed Chicken Breasts in White Wine Sauce)

Advance Preparation (1) Bone and flatten 8 breasts of chicken. Rub each with the cut side of a lemon and dip breasts into seasoned flour (1 cup flour, 1 teaspoon salt, and ¼ teaspoon white pepper). Shake off excess. Set aside until flour no longer looks dry, or a minimum of 20 minutes.

8 *single breasts of chicken*
½ *lemon*
1 *cup flour*
1 *teaspoon salt*
¼ *teaspoon white pepper*

(2) Assemble and have ready, 2 tablespoons each butter and oil, 2 tablespoons flour, ½ cup dry white wine, ½ cup condensed chicken broth with ½ teaspoon tarragon added, and 1 cup whipping cream.

2 *tablespoons butter*
2 *tablespoons oil*
2 *tablespoons flour*
½ *teaspoon salt*
½ *cup dry white wine*
½ *cup condensed chicken broth*
½ *teaspoon tarragon*
1 *cup whipping cream*

Final Preparation (1) *Sautéing Breasts* About 20 minutes prior to serving time, heat the butter and oil in a large skillet or electric frypan. Sauté the chicken breasts over moderate heat about 8 to 10 minutes on each side or until light golden brown. Remove breasts to heated serving platter.

(2) *Sauce au Vin Blanc* Add 2 tablespoon flour and ½ teaspoon salt to pan drippings. Cook one minute over moderate heat without browning. Stir in white wine and whisk until smooth. Whisk in the chicken broth and tarragon. When smooth, whisk in the heavy cream. Taste and add more salt and white pepper if necessary to sharpen flavor.

(3) Strain sauce and spoon over

breasts of chicken. At each end of platter, arrange a little nosegay of crisp watercress and several Brandied Apricots with Chutney.*

(4) *Brandied Apricots with Chutney* Open and drain one large can whole unpeeled apricots. Separate into halves and remove seeds. Allowing two halves per serving, fill each half with a spoonful of ready-made chutney. Place filled apricots in a baking pan and bake for 10 to 12 minutes. Remove from oven, drizzle with 2 tablespoons brandy and ignite. When flame has died down, arrange the apricots on platter with chicken breasts.

*Cook's Tip: When you aren't serving Soufflé aux Champignons in the same menu, garnish Breasts of Chicken Sautés with Sautéed Button Mushrooms, (Page 201).

1 can (1-pound 13-ounces) whole unpeeled apricots
1 small bottle ready-made chutney
2 tablespoons brandy

Soufflé aux Champignons (Mushroom Soufflé)

(1) *Mushrooms* Sauté 1 minced shallot in 2 tablespoons butter. Add ½ cup finely minced well-seasoned ham. Wash and trim ½ pound mushrooms. Mince the mushrooms with a stainless steel knife and add to ham mixture. Cook about 5 minutes. Reserve.

1 shallot, minced
2 tablespoons butter
½ cup minced ham
½ pound mushrooms, minced

(2) *Soufflé Base* Sauté 1 minced shallot in 4 tablespoons butter. Add 4 tablespoons flour and cook one minute without browning. Add 2 cups milk and whisk until smooth. Season

1 minced shallot
4 tablespoons butter
4 tablespoons flour
2 cups milk

with 1 teaspoon salt, a grating of nutmeg and ⅛ teaspoon white pepper.

(3) Combine mushrooms (Step 1), Soufflé Base and ½ cup shredded Swiss cheese. Cook, whisking steadily, until cheese is melted. Whisk in 6 egg yolks and continue cooking until smooth. Remove from heat and cool to lukewarm.

COOK'S TIP: Prepartion to this point can be done in the afternoon. Cover Soufflé Base and keep at room temperature. Place whites in large mixer bowl. Cover with plate and leave at room temperature. Forty-five minutes before serving proceed with Step 4.

(4) Add ½ teaspoon cream of tartar to 7 egg whites. Beat until stiff but not dry. Stir 1/3 of the whites into mushroom mixture until well blended. Fold in remaining whites gently.

(5) Butter a 2-quart soufflé dish and coat inside with grated Romano cheese. Spoon in the soufflé mixture. With a knife blade, cut a circle in top of soufflé to a depth of ½ inch, beginning ½ inch from edge of dish. Place in bottom one third of a 400-degree oven. Reduce heat immediately to 375 degrees and bake 35 minutes or until set. Serve as soon as possible.

1 teaspoon salt
A grating of nutmeg (1/8 teaspoon)
1/8 teaspoon white pepper
½ cup shredded Swiss cheese
6 egg yolks

7 egg whites
½ teaspoon cream of tartar
Dash of salt

1 tablespoon butter for soufflé dish
2 tablespoons grated Romano cheese

Broccoli Amandine
(Broccoli with Almonds)

(1) Dissolve 2 teaspoons instant chicken bouillon granules in ½ cup

2 teaspoons instant chicken bouillon granules

water in skillet. Arrange 2 packages partially thawed frozen broccoli spears in skillet. Flowerettes should be placed on outside edge of skillet with stalks converging in center. (Stalk are then exposed to more intense heat than the flowerettes and the whole spear cooks through evenly.) Simmer, uncovered, about 3 minutes. Turn spears over and continue simmering another 3 minutes. Test stalks for tenderness with the point of a knife. Drain and transfer to a heated serving dish.

(2) Place 3 tablespoons butter and ¼ cup slivered almonds in small skillet and stir constantly over moderate heat until butter and almonds are lightly browned. (Watch carefully, as the browning occurs all at once.) Stir in 1 tablespoon lemon juice and spoon over broccoli.

½ cup water
2 packages (10-ounce) frozen broccoli spears

3 tablespoons butter
¼ cup slivered almonds
1 tablespoon lemon juice

Strawberry Tart

Advance Preparation (1) *Sweet Tart Pastry* Place 1/3 cup butter in small mixer bowl. Cream in ¼ cup sugar. Beat in 1 cup sifted all-purpose flour, 1 egg yolk and ½ teaspoon vanilla. Gather mixture in hands and press into a ball.

(2) Butter the bottom of an 8-inch tart tin with removable bottom, and press the pastry evenly into the bottom and up the sides. Cut off excess dough even with the top edge. Return trimmings to bottom of crust and press until smooth.

1/3 cup butter
¼ cup sugar
1 cup all-purpose flour
1 egg yolk
½ teaspoon vanilla

(3) Bake at 350 degrees for 15 to 18 minutes, or until lightly browned. Remove from oven and, while hot, brush bottom with 1 tablespoon apricot jam.

(4) *Pudding Base* Blend 1/3 cup packaged vanilla pudding mix into 1 cup milk. Cook until mixture has come to a full boil. Remove from heat. Place a piece of waxed paper directly on top of pudding. Cool.

(5) *Strawberries* Wash and hull 2 cups whole strawberries of uniform size. Sprinkle with 3 to 4 tablespoons sugar and 2 tablespoons Kirsch.

(6) *Glaze** Combine ½ cup water, ¼ cup sugar, ¼ cup red currant jelly and 2 teaspoons arrowroot. Add 4 drops red food coloring. Place in saucepan and cook until mixture becomes clear.

Final Preparation Spoon the pudding into baked tart shell. Arrange the strawberries, points up, on pudding to fill shell completely. Spoon prepared glaze over strawberries, covering each completely. Refrigerate until serving time.

Optional The top may be decorated with a border of whipped cream rosettes before serving.

*COOK'S TIP: If you can locate Strawberry Junket Danish Dessert (pudding and pie filling) it can be substituted and makes a beautiful glaze. You will need one half of a 4-ounce package for one tart.

1 tablespoon apricot jam

1/3 cup packaged vanilla pudding mix
1 cup milk

2 cups strawberries
3 to 4 tablespoons sugar
2 tablespoons Kirsch

½ cup water
¼ cup sugar
¼ cup red currant jelly
2 teaspoons arrowroot
4 drops red food coloring

Oysters Rockefeller
Filets Mignons Flambés aux Champignons
Savory Green Beans
Assorted Cheeses
Chocolate Bavarian Cream Soufflé

With the Oysters, Chablis
With the Filets, red Burgundy, such as Gevry-Chambertin
With the cheese, red Burgundy, such as Richebourg

Legend has it that when Jules Alciatore of Antoine's in New Orleans invented his esteemed Oysters Rockefeller, he named the dish for the Rockefellers whom he presumed to be as rich as the dish. Some believe that he was searching for a national dish to give America which could favorably compete with the national first course of France, Escargots. Whatever his reasons, a belated, "Merci beaucoup, Monsieur Alciatore!"

Directions for preparing Oysters Rockefeller, using fresh oysters on the half-shell, are given in this menu. However, if you live inland and find that only shucked oysters are available, do not despair. You can collect shells from large white clams or small scallops and proceed with the recipe as you would for fresh oysters.

Traditionally, Oysters Rockefeller are served in dozen or half-dozen portions. Actually, you might prefer smaller portions of three or four. Locate interesting individual baking dishes such as sizzle steak platters, copper au gratin pans, or even disposable aluminum bakers. Fill the containers with rock salt to provide a stable base for the shells. I have even used my 18-inch paella pan to serve two dozen oysters in the living room during cocktails.

Men enjoy preparing Filets Mignons in a chafing dish. They like to flambé their steaks and enjoy the fun of making an expert sauce. This recipe was developed specifically for this purpose, but it is best to do only four fillets at one time in a chafing dish. If the man in your life really wants to try it, limit the guest list to four and use the same procedure as outlined here. These directions are for eight fillets to be prepared in the kitchen.

A cheese course is suggested following the entrée in this menu. The theory has been advanced that the cheese course was invented by the French to justify opening another bottle of wine. Undoubtedly, it does extend the lovely experience of dining in an unhurried atmosphere, with time to savor and contemplate the special qualities of an additional wine.

Since this entire menu is particularly appealing to men, you may as well go all the way and finish with chocolate. This delightful Bavarian cream can be made well ahead and will be greeted with unanimous broad grins when presented to "les gentilshommes."

Oysters Rockefeller

Advance Preparation (1) Sauté 8 strips bacon until crisp. Remove from pan, crumble and reserve. Pour off excess bacon fat and add ½ cup butter to pan. Add 4 pressed cloves garlic, and 1 cup each finely minced fresh spinach, parsley and green onion. Cook until vegetables are limp. Add 3 teaspoons Worcestershire sauce, 2 tabelspoons Pernod, a dash Tabasco, 1 teaspoon salt and a little freshly ground black pepper. Transfer to top of blender and add reserved bacon. Blend until smooth and stir in 1 cup fine bread crumbs.

(2) Fill 8 pie pans (or other flat containers of uniform size) with rock salt and arrange 6 oysters on the half-shell in each.

COOK'S TIP: To open oysters at home, scrub until clean with brush and place on baking sheet. Place in a 400-degree oven for 5 minutes. Remove from oven and drop into ice water. They

8 strips bacon
½ cup butter
4 cloves garlic
1 cup minced fresh spinach
1 cup minced parsley
1 cup minced green onion
3 teaspoons Worcestershire sauce
2 tablespoons Pernod
Dash Tabasco
1 teaspoon salt
Freshly ground black pepper as desired
1 cup fine bread crumbs

4-5 pounds rock salt
48 oysters

can then be easily opened with a kitchen knife.

(3) Cover each oyster completely with prepared topping. Reserve until 20 minutes before serving time.

Final Preparation Place oysters in preheated 400-degree oven for 15 minutes, or until bubbling hot and lightly browned. Serve at once with a wedge of lemon per serving.

8 wedges fresh lemon

Filets Mignons Flambes aux Champignons (Flambeed Fillets with Mushroom Sauce)

Advance Preparation (1) Have eight 1-inch fillets cut from choice of prime tenderloin of beef. Remove from refrigerator one hour prior to cooking. Rub each fillet with olive oil and pat a little freshly ground black pepper into the surface of each.

8 filets mignons, 1-inch thick
Olive oil
Freshly ground black pepper

(2) Assemble 4 tablespoons cognac, ¼ cup red wine, 4 tablespoons butter, 1 minced shallot and ½ pound sliced mushrooms. (Slice from stem through cap.) Keep ingredients in individual containers and reserve on a tray near cooking area.

4 tablespoons cognac
¼ cup red wine
4 tablespoons butter
1 shallot, minced
½ pound mushrooms, sliced

(3) *Stock and Seasonings* Combine in a small pitcher 2 teaspoons B.V., ½ cup water, 1 teaspoon Worcestershire sauce, ½ teaspoon tarragon, ½ teaspoon salt and 1 teaspoon arrowroot.

2 teaspoon B.V. (beefer-upper)
½ cup water
1 teaspoon Worcestershire sauce
½ teaspoon tarragon
½ teaspoon salt
1 teaspoon arrowroot

(4) *Toast* Brush 3-inch rounds of pumpernickel rye bread with butter and toast until crisp in a 350-degree

oven, turning once. Place on heated serving platter and keep in warm oven.

Final Preparation (1) *Fillets* Heat 2 tablespoons butter in a large flat skillet or electric frypan. Fry steaks about 2 minutes on each side. The heat should be as high as possible without burning butter. Heat the cognac, ignite and pour over steaks while still in frypan. Transfer steaks to toast rounds.

(2) *Mushroom Sauce* Turn heat to highest setting and add remaining 2 tablespoons butter to frypan. Sauté the minced shallot briefly. Add mushrooms and cook through quickly. Add red wine and cook rapidly to exhaust alcohol. Add contents of pitcher containing seasoning mixture and cook until thickened and mushrooms are glazed. Spoon the sauce over steaks immediately and garnish with sprigs of watercress or finely minced parsley.

8 (3-inch) rounds pumpernickel rye bread, toasted

Several sprigs crisp water cress, or 2 tablespoons minced parsley

Savory Green Beans
Place 2 packages partially thawed whole green beans in skillet with 1 teaspoon summer savory, 1 tablespoon butter and ¼ cup water. Cook gently, uncovered, until all water is evaporated. Add one more tablespoon butter, turn heat up. Toss beans over high heat until glazed. Sprinkle with salt to taste just prior to serving.

2 packages (9-ounce) whole green beans
1 teaspoon summer savory
1 tablespoon butter
¼ cup water
1 tablespoon butter
Salt to taste

Cheese Board

On your most attractive cutting board arrange three or more of the soft French cheeses such as Brie, Camembert, Bonbel, Pont l'Evêque, Port Salut, Gourmandise or Roquefort. Allow cheese to stand at room temperature for 1 hour prior to serving. Remove the dinner plates and supply each guest with a fruit plate. Pass the cheese board. You may serve thinly sliced French bread and butter, but avoid salted crackers as cheese usually is salty enough.

COOK'S TIP: On some occasions you may choose to serve a basket of fresh fruit with cheeses such as these. At these times you may omit any other dessert course.

SELECT FROM:
Brie
Camembert
Bonbel
Pont l'Evêque
Port Salut
Gourmandise
Roquefort
Sliced French bread
Butter

Chocolate Bavarian Soufflé

Advance Preparation (1) Combine in top of double boiler, 2 envelopes unflavored gelatin, ½ cup sugar and ¼ teaspoon salt. Separate 4 eggs and beat the yolks into 2 cups milk. Add to gelatin mixture. Add 2 cups semi-sweet chocolate bits and cook mixture over simmering water, stirring constantly, until chocolate has melted. Remove from heat and beat until chocolate is well blended. Cool until mixture is consistency of unbeaten egg white. Stir in 2 tablespoons orange-flavored liqueur.

(2) Beat the 4 egg whites with ¼

2 envelopes unflavored gelatin (2 tablespoons)
½ cup sugar
¼ teaspoon salt
4 eggs, separated
2 cups milk
2 cups semi-sweet chocolate bits
2 tablespoons orange liqueur

teaspoon cream of tartar until frothy. Gradually add ½ cup sugar, continuing to beat until firm glossy peaks have formed. Fold into chocolate mixture.
(3) Beat 1 cup whipping cream until thick and fairly stiff. Fold into chocolate mixture.
(4) Collar a 4-cup soufflé dish and spoon mixture into dish. Chill 3 to 4 hours.
Final Preparation At serving time, remove collar and decorate top of the dessert with rosettes of whipped cream and chocolate curls.

4 egg whites (from Step 1)
¼ teaspoon cream of tartar
½ cup sugar

1 cup whipping cream

How to collar soufflé dish (Page 40)

½ cup whipping cream
Chocolate curls

Escargots à la Bourguignonne
Crown Roast of Lamb with Sautéed Button Mushrooms
Greek-Style Rice with Spinach
Bibb Lettuce Mimosa
Cold Lemon Soufflé

With the Escargots, Pouilly-Fuissé or White Graves
With the Lamb, red Bordeaux:
St. Emilion, Margaux, or Pomerol

When you want to entertain a few choice friends who are avowed lovers of lamb, your choice of cut might be determined by the ease with which you can expect to prepare it. Although the regal crown roast might appear to be the most difficult, it is very probably the most simple.

A crown roast is made from two or three rib sections, known as racks. Each will contain from six to eight chops. The two-rack crown is the best looking, but it serves only six persons. If you are planning to serve eight persons ask for a three-rack crown and locate a platter large enough to hold it before you start.

Preparation is simplicity itself, as the roast has only to be rubbed with oil, salt, pepper and herbs. Thyme and rosemary are specifically recommended to bring out the best natural flavors of lamb. This recipe takes the guesswork out of timing, whether you choose the two or three-rack roast. It also allows for a holding period during which you can place the accompanying dishes in a warm oven and serve your first course of Escargots.

The most rewarding part of eating escargots is mopping up the garlic butter in the bottom of the baking dish with a good French bread. Baguettes from Paris, flown in by jet, are available in many grocery freezer cases and are well worth seeking out for this purpose. With the escargots you might enjoy serving a dry white Burgundy such as Pouilly-Fuissé or a white Graves.

This presentation of the crown roast is a handsome sight. The center is filled with button mushrooms and the base is decorated with tiny baked tomatoes and crisp sprigs of watercress.

The Greek-style rice presented with lamb in this menu is also very good with poultry dishes and pork roasts. If desired, it could be used as an alternate filling for the crown roast.

When the host begins to carve, it will be so easy that he may be overcome with feelings of expertise. (The butcher has taken the treachery out of carving by partially severing each rib.) If he selects a fine red Bordeaux wine to serve with the lamb, he will also be praised for his exquisite good taste. This is continental dining at its finest!

Ecargots à la Bourguignonne
(Snails Burgundy Style)

Advance Preparation (1) Allowing 6 snails per person, drop the shells into boiling water. Let stand a few minutes. Remove shells from water and turn to drain.	*4 dozen snail shells*
(2) *Snail Butter* Cream together 1 pound butter, ¼ cup finely minced	*1 pound butter* *¼ cup finely minced shallots*

shallot and ½ cup finely minced parsley. Add 3 pressed cloves garlic, 1 teaspoon basil, 1 teaspoon salt, ½ teaspoon freshly ground black pepper and the juice of 1 lemon.

(3) *Snails* Open and drain 4 dozen snails. Rinse under cool running water and drain on paper towels.

(4) *Assembly* Place a little butter in each shell. Insert a snail and seal with additional butter. Refrigerate until needed.

Final Preparation Preheat oven to 400 degrees. Arrange snails on individual baking dishes and pour a little dry white wine or vermouth in bottom of each dish. Bake about 12 minutes or until bubbling hot. Transfer baking dishes to service plates. Serve with fresh, crusty French bread.

COOK'S TIP: In order to accumulate shells for Escargots, you should buy the package which contains the snails in a can. The neccessary number of shells is in a see-through tube attached to the can. By all means, save the shells! Next time you prepare Escargots, you will only have to buy the snails.

½ cup finely minced parsley
3 cloves garlic, pressed
1 teaspoon basil
1 teaspoon salt
½ teaspoon freshly ground black pepper
Juice of 1 lemon (3-4 tablespoons)

4 dozen canned snails

Dry white wine, or dry vermouth for baking dishes
1 loaf French bread, sliced

Crown Roast of Lamb with Sautéed Button Mushrooms

Advance Preparation (1) *Lamb* Have the butcher prepare a crown roast (about 4 to 5 pounds) from a double rack of lamb. Yield: 2 to 3 chops per serving for six persons. To serve eight

1 crown roast of lamb, about 4 to 5 pounds, or 12 to 14 chops

persons, have crown made from 3 racks of lamb.

(2) One hour prior to roasting time, rub the roast with French olive oil. Combine 1 teaspoon each salt, thyme, and rosemary. Add ½ teaspoon freshly ground black pepper. Rub into surface of crown, inside and out. Allow to stand 1 hour.

1 tablespoon French olive oil
1 teaspoon salt
1 teaspoon thyme
1 teaspoon rosemary
Freshly ground black pepper

(3) *Mushrooms* Wash 2 pounds button mushrooms quickly in cold water. Cut the stems off evenly with the underside of cap. Wipe dry with paper towels to remove loose skin and any of the remaining compost in which they are grown.

Sauté 2 minced shallots in 4 tablespoons butter in a 15-inch skillet. Remove from heat and add the mushrooms. Toss to coat with butter. Reserve.

2 pounds fresh button mushrooms
4 tablespoons butter
2 shallots, minced
Salt to taste
2 to 3 cherry tomatoes per serving
½ recipe Filling for Tomatoes Niçoises (Page 146)

(4) *Tiny Tomatoes Niçoices* Cut top one-fourth off each of 12 to 18 cherry tomatoes. Carefully hollow out and sprinkle insides of tomatoes with salt. Turn upside down to drain.

Prepare one-half recipe of crumb filling for Tomatoes Niçoises (Page 146). Fill cherry tomatoes. Place tomatoes in a baking dish. Bake in the oven with lamb during last 20 minutes baking time.

Final Preparation (1) Place crown roast on rack in roaster in a 375-degree oven. Roast for 1 hour for pink lamb; 1 hour and 10 minutes for more well done. Transfer lamb to a heated serving platter, cover loosely, and let stand 15 minutes before carving. Lamb may also be held in a warm oven for up to half an hour.

(2) Return mushrooms to moderate heat and cook while shaking pan and tossing until all natural juices have been reabsorbed. Sprinkle lightly with salt during sautéing. When mushrooms are delicately browned, cease cooking and spoon them into center of crown roast. Sprinkle 2 tablespoons finely minced parsley over mushrooms. Decorate chops with paper frills.* Arrange prepared Tiny Tomatoes Niçoises around base of roast. Insert sprigs of crisp watercress at random.

*COOK'S TIP: If you are unable to locate paper frills, you may make your own. Cut 2½-inch squares of white paper. Fold in half and with kitchen shears make ¼-inch cuts very close together on the folded side. Wrap the un-cut portion around the round handle of a wooden spoon, slip off and glue together, forming a fringed circle. Hold with paper clips until glue dries.

2 tablespoons minced parsley
1 bunch watercress
1 paper frill per chop

Greek-Style Rice with Spinach

(1) Sauté 1 medium diced onion in ¼ cup French olive oil. Add 1½ cups converted rice and stir until rice is well coated with oil. Transfer to 6-cup oven-to-table baking dish.

(2) Dissolve 6 chicken bouillon cubes in 3 cups boiling water and add ½ teaspoon sage. Pour over rice. Ar-

1 medium onion, diced
¼ cup French olive oil
1½ cups converted rice

6 chicken bouillon cubes
3 cups boiling water
½ teaspoon sage

range one (10-ounce) package partially thawed frozen chopped spinach on top of rice.
(3) Cover dish and bake at 375 degrees for 25 minutes or until all liquid is absorbed.* Uncover and stir spinach into rice.

*COOK'S TIP: If oven space is limited, you may cook this rice, covered, in a skillet, on top of the stove.

1 package (10-ounce) frozen chopped spinach, partially thawed

Bibb Lettuce Mimosa
Advance Preparation (1) Select 8 perfect heads of Bibb lettuce. Wash gently by submerging in large amount of cold water. Holding by the stem, shake off excess water. Lay on large kitchen towels and roll. Refrigerate until needed.
(2) Prepare 1 recipe Sauce Vinaigrette aux Fines Herbes and 1 recipe Mimosa Garnish.
Final Preparation and Service Place whole heads of lettuce on individual chilled salad plates. Drizzle with Sauce Vinaigrette. Sprinkle with salt. Scatter Mimosa Garnish on top.

8 heads Bibb lettuce

1 recipe Sauce Vinaigrette aux Fines Herbes (Page 24)
1 recipe Mimosa Garnish (Page 45)
Salt to taste

Cold Lemon Soufflé
Advance Preparation (1) Dissolve 2 envelopes unflavored gelatin in ½ cup cold water in top of stainless or enameled double boiler. Separate 6 eggs. Reserve whites. Beat the yolks until light lemon color and add ½ cup

2 envelopes (2 tablespoons) unflavored gelatin
½ cup cold water
6 eggs, separated
½ cup sugar
½ cup lemon juice

sugar and ½ cup lemon juice. Add to gelatin mixture in double boiler. Cook over simmering water, whisking steadily with stainless wire whisk, until mixture is smooth and slightly thickened (about 8 minutes). Remove from heat and cool until mixture is cool to the touch.

COOK'S TIP: The cooling may be hastened by placing double boiler over ice water. Stir constantly with whisk and test temperature often. Mixture should be just free of warmth and attaining the consistency of unbeaten egg white. If mixture becomes too thick or begins to lump, you must place the double boiler over warm water and whisk until smooth. Begin cooling process again.

(2) Beat 6 egg whites, a dash of salt and ½ teaspoon cream of tartar until frothy. Continue beating while gradually adding ½ cup sugar. Cease beating when stiff glossy peaks have formed. Fold yolk mixture into whites.

6 egg whites (from Step 1)
Dash of salt
½ teaspoon cream of tartar
½ cup sugar

(3) *Whipped Cream* Beat 1 cup whipping cream until thickened but not completely stiff. Fold into combined egg mixtures.

1 cup whipping cream

Final Preparation (1) Butter the bottom of an 8-inch spring form pan. Line the sides with ladyfingers, standing them upright around outside edge of pan. Spoon the soufflé mixture into pan and refrigerate until serving time, or a minimum of 4 hours.

2 dozen ladyfingers

(2) *Service* Loosen ladyfingers from edge of pan with the tip of knife, and carefully slip off outside of pan.
Garnish Cut a ⅛-inch slice of lemon and remove seeds. Make a cut through the rind to center of slice. Twisting lemon into an "S" shape, place it in center of soufflé and arrange a tiny sprig of mint in each curve of "S". Cut soufflé into wedges with a stainless steel knife, to serve.

Slice of lemon
2 sprigs mint

COOK'S TIP: Do use a stainless steel whisk and knife. The strong acidity of lemon will transmit a metallic flavor to the soufflé if tin or carbon steel is used.

INDEX

Almond Cookies, 107
Almond Macaroons, 8
Alsatian Green Beans, 166
Antipasto Piatto Grande, 148
Antipasto Salad, Garden Relish, 137
Apple Cake, Swedish, 184
Appetizers (see also **Soups**)
    Antipasto Piatte Grande, 148
    Artichokes with Tarragon
      Mayonnaise, 143
    Asaparagus Vinaigrette, 44
    Beef Teriyaki on Skewers, 94
    Beets Vinaigrette, 49
    Carrots Vinaigrette, 49
    Caviar and Blini, 186
    Celeriac in Caper Sauce, 49
    Chicken Livers in Chopped Aspic, 181
    Chili con Queso and Tostadas, 120
    Chinese Garlic Spareribs, 104
    Cucumbers in Sour Cream, 49, 76
    Deviled Eggs and Caviar, 75
    Deviled Ham on Rye, 163
    Eggs in Mayonnaise, 48
    Escargots a la Bourgignonne, 199
    French Potato Salad, 157
    Garden Relish Antipasto Salad, 137
    Green Beans Vinaigrette, 156
    Marinated Mushroom Caps, 48
    Oysters Rockefeller, 194
    Pirozhky, 78
    Raclette, 28
    Rillettes de Tours, 173
    Salade Olivier, 75
    Seviche, 115
    Shrimp Toast, 99
    Tabouleh, 69
    Tiny Lobster Sandwiches, 163
    Tomato Salad, 157
    Tostadas con Queso, 125
    Tuna Vinaigrette with Anchovies, 157
    Watercress Roll-Ups, 163
    White Bean Salad, 76
    Zakusky, 74
Aromatic Rice Pilau, 82
Arroz Blanco, 122
Artichokes with Tarragon Mayonnaise, 143
Asaparagus Vinaigrette, 44
Assorted Canapes, 163
Avocado Egg-Flower Soup, 89

Beef and Pea Pods in Oyster Sauce, 105
Beef Teriyaki on Skewers, 94
Beets Vinaigrette, 49
Berliner Kransers, Ragna Oas, 7

Beverages
    Chambraise on the Rocks, 10
    Cognac Chantilly (coffee), 9
    Iced Tomato Juice Cocktail, 15
    Pineapple Cooler, 6
    Sangria, White Wine, 112
Bibb Lettuce Mimosa, 203
Biscuit Tortoni, 135
Black Cherry Cheesecake, 171
Blender Vinaigrette a la Moutarde, 30
Blueberries in Sour Cream, 61
Boeuf Bourguignon, 174
Boiled New Potatoes, 171
Borsch, Mrs. Conlin's Best, 77
Bouillabaisse, 158
Braised Celery and Zucchini, 140
Breads
    Brioche, 3
    Caraway Rye, Toasted, 184
    French, 159
    Garlic, Toasted, 141
    Melba Toast, Homemade, 182
    Puris, 83
    Sour Cream Coffee Cake, 13
Breasts of Chicken Saute,
  Sauce au Vin Blanc, 188
Brioche, 3
Broccoli Amandine, 190
Buttered Mushroom-Spaghetti, 151
Buttered New Potatoes, 171

Cakes
    Black Cherry Cheesecake, 171
    Gateau du Jour, 26
    Pineapple Upsidedown Cake Roll, 35
    Sour Cream Coffee Cake, 13
    Sultana, 78
    Swedish Apple, 184
Canapes (See **Appetizers**)
Cannelloni, 50
Caper Sauce, 49
Caraway Rye Bread, Toasted, 184
Carne Asada, 125
Carrots Vinaigrette, 49
Caviar and Blini, 186
Celeriac in Caper Sauce, 49
Celestial Chicken Salad, 101
Chambraise on the Rocks, 10
Checklist for Salad Greens, 29
Cheese and Cheese Dishes
    Cheese Board, 197
    Cheese Souffle, 59
    Quiche Lorraine, Quick, 23
    Quiche Lorraine, Standard, 22
    Raclette, 28
Cheese Board, 197
Cheese Souffle, 59
Chef's Salad Bar, 29
Chicken and Black Mushrooms, 104
Chili con Queso and Tostadas, 120
Chinese Garlic Spareribs, 104
Chocolate Bavarian Souffle, 197
Chocolate Raspberry Torte, 31
Chocolate Sauce, 177
Choucroute Garnie, 170
Cinnamon-Fried Bananas with
  Apricot Yoghurt, 84
Coeur a la Creme with Strawberries, 56
Coffee Cake
    Brioche, 3
    Sour Cream, 13
Cognac Chantilly, 9
Cookies
    Almond, 107
    Almond Macaroons, 8
    Berliner Kransers, Ragna Oas, 7
    Swedish Butter Balls, 7
Coq-Au-Vin, 164
Coquilles Saint-Jacques Florentine, 45
Cottage Scrambled Eggs, 3
Crepes, How to Fry, 50
Crepes Suzette, 167
Croque Monsieur, 6
Cucumbers in Rice Wine Vinegar, 91
Cucumbers in Sour Cream, 49, 76
Cucumber Vichyssoise, 54
Curried Chicken-Lychee Salad, 38

Deluxe Salad, California Style, 34
Desserts
    Chocolate Raspberry Torte, 31
    Coeur á la Creme with Strawberries, 56
    Cognac Chantilly, 9
    Crepes, How to Fry, 50
    Crepes Suzette, 167
    Flan con Salsa Caramelo, 67
    Flan, Spiced Pumpkin, 118
    Gingered Cream Chantilly, 36
    Marsala Pudding with Meringue, 146
    Pots-de-Creme au Chocolat, 52

Profiteroles au Chocolat, 176
Zabaglione, 153
Desserts, Frozen
Biscuit, Tortoni, 135
Green Tea Sherbet, 91
Ice Cream with Ginger Marmalade, 92
Ice Cream with
  Rum-Currant Sauce, 123
Melon and Orange Sherbet, 72
Deviled Eggs and Caviar, 75
Duchess Potato Souffle, 183

Eggs
Benedict, 15
Cottage Scrambled, 3
Deviled, with Caviar, 75
Frittata, Green Pepper, 134
Hard-Cooked, 39
Huevos Rancheros, 113
in Mayonnaise, 48
Scrambled, Cottage Style, 3
Enchiladas, Sour Cream Chicken, 126
Ensalada con Guacamole, 122
Escargots a la Bourgigonne, 199

Fish and Seafood
Bouillabaisse, 158
Coquilles Saint-Jacques Florentine, 45
Escargots a la Bourgignonne, 199
Gazpacho, 64
Oysters Rockefeller, 194
Seviche, 115
Shrimp Toast, 99
Sweet and Sour Shrimp, 106
Tempura, 95
Flan con Salsa Caramelo, 67
Flan, Spiced Pumpkin, 118
Florentine Meatballs, 144
French Bread, Homemade, 159
French Onion Soup, 33
French-Style Green Peas, 12
Frittata, Green Pepper, 134
Fruits and Fruit Desserts
Blueberries in Sour Cream, 61
Cinnamon-fried Bananas with
  Apricot Yoghurt, 84
Grenadine Citrus Cup, 2
Lychees and Melon in
  Japanese Plum Wine, 97
Macedonia de Frutta al Marsala, 141

Mangos on Ice, 128
Melon and Orange Sherbet, 72
Melon and Tropical Fruit Platter, 113
Oranges Grand Marnier, 17
Oriental Fruits in Gingered Honey, 102
Peaches in Raspberry Sauce, 46
Pineapple Cooler, 6
Pineapple-meringue au Rhum, 128
Prunes a la Alice B. Toklas, 17
Scalloped Apples, 6
Strawberry Tart, 191

Garden Relish Antipasto Salad, 137
Garlic Bread, Toasted, 141
Gateau du Jour, 26
Gazpacho, 64
Ginger, 36
Gingered Chicken Broth, 38
Gingered Crème Chantilly, 36
Greek-style Rice with Spinach, 202
Green Beans Vinaigrette, 156
Green Beans with Savory, 196
Green Goddess Dressing, 30
Green Pepper Frittata, 134
Green Tea Sherbet, 91
Grenadine Citrus Cup, 2

Ham and Asparagus Roulades, 55
Herbed Beef Broth, 162
Huevos Rancheros, 113

Ice Cream with Ginger Marmalade, 92
Ice Cream with Rum-Currant Sauce, 123
Iced Tomato Juice Cocktail, 15
Indonesian Pork Sates, 80
Insalata Verde, 152

Lamb, Crown Roast with
  Sauteed Button Mushrooms, 200
Lamb Curry, 81
Lamb Shish Kebab, 70
Lasagne Bolognese, 138
Lemon-Curry Vinaigrette, 176
Lemon-Glazed Carrots, 12
Lemon Souffle, Cold, 203
Little Jars of Jam, 4
Lychees and Melon in
  Japanese Plum Wine, 97

Macedonia de Frutta al Marsala, 141

Mangos on Ice, 128
Marinated Mushroom Caps, 48
Marsala Pudding with Meringue, 146
Meats
   Beef
      Beef and Pea Pods
         in Oyster Sauce, 105
      Beef Teriyaki on Skewers, 94
      Boeuf Bourguignon, 174
      Carne Asada, 125
      Filet Mignon, 195
      Lasagne Bolognese, 138
      Meatballs, Florentine, 144
      Mexican Green Peppers con
         Salsa de Tomate, 121
      Pirozhky, 78
      Sukiyaki, 89
   Ham
      Ham and Asparagus Roulades, 55
      Sherried Ham and Turkey, 10
   Lamb
      Crown Roast of Lamb with
         Sautéed Button Mushrooms, 200
      Lamb Curry, 81
      Lamb Shish Kebab, 70
   Pork
      Chaucroute Garnie, 170
      Chinese Garlic Spareribs, 104
      Indonesian Pork Sates, 80
      Oven-Fried Farm Sausage, 3
      Pork-Fried Rice, 100
      Pork Loin Roast
         and Red Cabbage, 182
      Rillettes de Tours, 173
      Sausage, Sweet Roasted, 135
   Veal
      Veal Parmigiana, 149
Melba Toast, Homemade, 182
Melon and Orange Sherbet, 72
Melon and Tropical Fruit Platter, 113
Mexican Green Peppers
   con Salsa de Tomate, 121
Middle Eastern Pilaf, 71
Mimosa Garnish, 45
Mixed Grilled Vegetables, 60
Minestrone with Pesto Sauce, 133

Oranges Grand Marnier, 17
Orange Souffle, Cold, 39
Oriental Fruits in Gingered Honey, 102

Oven-Fried Farm Sausage, 3
Oven-Grilled Eggplant and Tomato, 71
Oysters Rockefeller, 194

Paella a la Valenciana, 65
Peaches in Raspberry Sauce, 46
Pesto Sauce, 134
Petits Pois Pontet Canet, 52
Pineapple Cooler, 6
Pineapple Meringue au Rhum, 128
Pineapple Upside-Down Cake Roll, 35
Pirozhky, 78
Pork Fried Rice, 100
Pork Loin Roast and Red Cabbage, 182
Potato Souffle, Duchess, 183
Pots-de-Creme au Chocolat, 52
Poultry
   Breasts of Chicken Sautes,
      Sauce au Vin Blanc, 188
   Celestial Chicken Salad, 101
   Chicken and Black Mushrooms, 104
   Chicken Tacos, Soft, 116
   Coq-au-Vin, 164
   Paella a la Valenciana, 65
   Rock Cornish Game Hens Teriyaki, 99
   Sherried Ham and Turkey, 10
   Sour Cream Chicken Enchiladas, 126
Profiteroles au Chocolat, 176
Prunes a la Alice B. Toklas, 17
Puris, 83

Quiche Lorraine
   Quick Method, 23
   Standard Method, 22

Raclette, 28
Rice and Pastas
   Aromatic Rice Pilau, 82
   Arroz Blanco, 122
   Buttered Mushroom-Spaghetti, 151
   Cannelloni, 50
   Greek-Style Rice with Spinach, 202
   Middle Eastern Pilaf, 71
   Paella, 65
   Pork Fried Rice, 100
   Rice, Steamed, 91
   Risi Bisi, 145
   Riz Meringue, 160
   Spaghetti, Buttered Mushrooms, 151
Rice, Steamed, 91

Rillettes de Tours, 173
Risi Bisi, 145
Riz Meringue, 160
Rock Cornish Game Hens Teriyaki, 99
Roquefort Sour Cream Dressing, 31

Salad Dressings
    Blender Vinaigrette a la Moutarde, 30
    Green Goddess, 30
    Italian Vinaigrette, 152
    Lemon-Curry, 176
    Roquefort Sour Cream, 31
    Tarragon Mayonnaise, 144
    Vinaigrette aux Fines Herbes, 24
Salade de Saison, 166
Salade Nicoise, 24
Salade Olivier, 75
Salads
    Bibb Lettuce Mimosa, 203
    Celestial Chicken, 101
    Checklist for Salad Greens, 29
    Chef's Salad Bar, 29
    Cucumbers in Rice Wine Vinegar, 91
    Cucumbers in Sour Cream, 49, 76
    Curried Chicken-Lychee, 38
    Deluxe, California Style, 34
    Ensalada con Guacamole, 122
    Garden Relish Antipasto, 137
    Insalata Verde, 152
    Salade de Saison, 166
    Salade Nicoise, 24
    Salade Olivier, 25
    Tabouleh, 69
    White Bean, 76
        with Lemon-Curry Vinaigrette, 176
Sangria, White Wine, 112
Sauce au Vin Blanc, 188
Sauce Bearnaise, 55
Sauce Mornay, 51
Sauce Vinaigrette aux Fines Herbes, 24
Sausage, Sweet Roasted, 135
Savory Green Beans, 196
Scalloped Apples, 6
Seviche, 115
Sherbet
    Green Tea, 91
    Melon and Orange, 72
Sherried Beef Broth on the Rocks, 59
Sherried Ham and Turkey, 10
Shrimp and Assorted

    Vegetables Tempura, 95
Shrimp Toast, 99
Soft Chicken Tacos, 116
Souffle aux Champignons, 189
Souffles
    aux Champignons, 189
    Cheese, 59
    Chocolate Bavarian, 197
    Lemon, Cold, 203
    Orange, Cold, 39
    Potato, 183
Soups
    Avocado Egg-Flower, 89
    Borsch, Mrs. Conlin's Best, 77
    Bouillabaisse, 158
    Cucumber Vichyssoise, 54
    French Onion, 33
    Gazpacho, 64
    Gingered Chicken Broth, 38
    Herbed Beef Broth, 162
    Minestrone with Pesto Sauce, 133
    Sherried Beef Broth on the Rocks, 59
    Tomato-Corn Chowder, 169
Sour Cream Chicken Enchiladas, 126
Sour Cream Coffee Cake, 13
Spaghetti, Buttered Mushroom, 151
Spiced Pumpkin Flan, 118
Strawberry Sauce, 57
Strawberry Tart, 191
Sukiyaki, 89
Sultana Cake, 78
Swedish Apple Cake, 184
Swedish Butter Balls, 7
Sweet and Sour Shrimp, 106
Sweet Roasted Sausage, 135

Tabouleh, 69
Tacos, Soft Chicken, 116
Tarragon Mayonnaise, 144
Tempura, 95
Tomato-Corn Chowder, 169
Tomatoes Nicoises, 146
Tostadas con Frijoles, 118
Tostadas con Queso, 125

Veal Parmigiana, 149
Vegetables
    Artichokes with
        Tarragon Mayonnaise, 143
    Asparagus Vinaigrette, 44

Beets Vinaigrette, 49
Broccoli Amandine, 190
Carrots, Lemon-Glazed, 12
Carrots Vinaigrette, 49
Celeriac in Caper Sauce, 49
Celery and Zucchini, Braised, 140
Cucumbers in Rice Wine Vinegar, 91
Cucumbers in Sour Cream, 49, 76
French-Style Green Peas, 12
Green Beans, Alsatian, 166
Green Beans with Savory, 196
Mexican Green Peppers con Salsa de Tomate, 121
Mixed Grilled Vegetables, 60
Mushroom Caps, Marinated, 48

Oven-Grilled Eggplant and Tomato, 71
Petits Pois Pontent Canet, 52
Potatoes Boiled, New, 171
Potato Souffle, Duchess, 183
Souffle aux Champignons, 189
Tomatoes Nicoises, 146
Vegetable-Herb Bouquet, 170
Vinaigrette, aux Fines Herbes, 24

White Bean Salad, 76
White Wine Sangria, 112

Zabaglione, 153
Zakusky, 74